The Ebb and Flow of Battle

The Ebb and Flow of Battle

P. J. CAMPBELL

OXFORD UNIVERSITY PRESS

OXFORD NEW YORK MELBOURNE

1979

Oxford University Press, Walton Street, Oxford OX2 6DP

OXFORD LONDON GLASGOW
NEW YORK TORONTO MELBOURNE WELLINGTON
KUALA LUMPUR SINGAPORE JAKARTA HONG KONG TOKYO
DELHI BOMBAY CALCUTTA MADRAS KARACHI
NAIROBI DAR ES SALAAM CAPE TOWN

© P. J. Campbell 1977

First published in Great Britain 1977 by Hamish
Hamilton Ltd., 90 Great Russell Street,
London WC1B 3PT. First issued as an Oxford
University Press Paperback 1979.

British Library Cataloguing in Publication Data

Campbell, P J
  The ebb and flow of battle.
  1. Great Britain. Army. Fifth Army – History
  2. European War, 1914–18 – Campaigns –
Western
  I. Title
  940.4′34′0924   D547.F/   79–40244
  ISBN 0–19–281262–9

Printed in Great Britain by
REDWOOD BURN LIMITED
Trowbridge & Esher

To the men with whom I served
in the Army-Brigade, Royal Field Artillery,
of this story: and to today's young men
who have equally great difficulties
to overcome

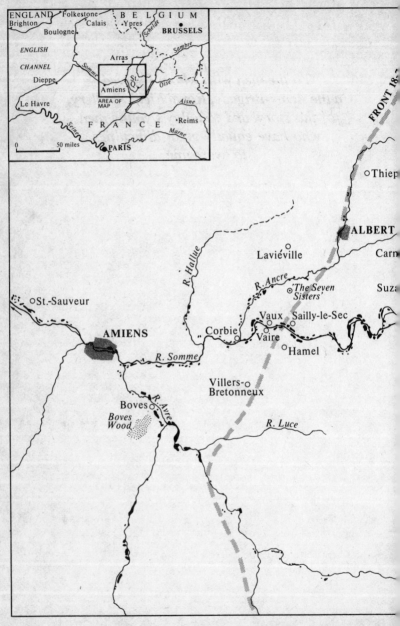

Retreat and final advance

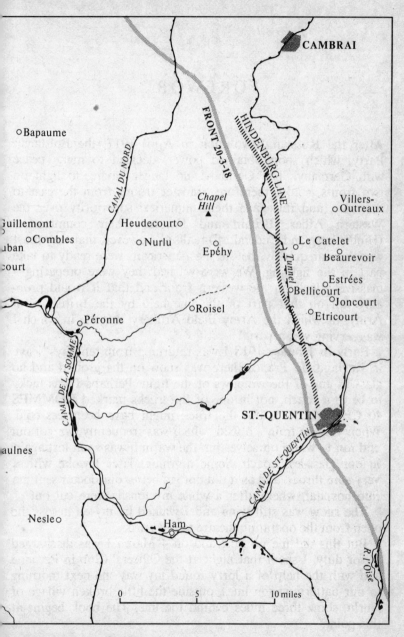

CAMBRAI

○Bapaume

CANAL DU NORD

FRONT 20-3-18

HINDENBURG LINE

Chapel Hill ▲

Villers-
○Outreaux

Guillemont

○Combles

Heudecourt○

Nurlu

Epéhy

○Le Catelet

Beaurevoir

Tunnel

Estrées

○Bellicourt

Joncourt

○Etricourt

Roisel

uban

court

○Péronne

CANAL DE LA SOMME

ST.–QUENTIN

aulnes

CANAL DE ST-QUENTIN

Nesle○

Ham

R. l'Oise

0   5   10 miles

of the Western Front, 1918

FOREWORD

After the Russian Revolution in April 1917, the Bolshevik Party, which soon obtained power, decided to make peace with Germany. The Germans, no longer having to fight on two fronts, could, therefore, transfer troops from the east to the west, and this gave them numerical superiority over the Western Allies, Britain and France. Their commanders (Hindenburg and Ludendorff) realised, however, that they must win the war quickly, before the Americans were ready to take part in the fighting. We were warned they were preparing a massive attack on the western front and that it would probably fall on that part of the line held by the British Fifth Army, of which the Army Field Artillery Brigade in which I was serving was a part.

Early in January 1918 I was returning from ten days' leave in England. In France there was snow on the ground and no glass in any of the windows of the train. Perhaps I was lucky to be in a coach, not in one of the trucks marked HOMMES 40 CHEVAUX 8, but the truck might have been less cold. Whenever the train stopped, which was frequently, we got out and ran to warm ourselves but the warmth was soon lost again in our glass-less coach. Some mornings later I woke with a very sore throat, and as it did not get better our doctor sent me into hospital, where after a while my tonsils were cut out.

The snow was still lying and I walked by myself across the open from the operating theatre to my ward.

But this did me no hurt and on 4 March I was discharged fit for duty. I spent that night at the Officers' Club in Peronne and with the help of a lorry found my way the next morning to our battery wagon lines, outside the little broken village of Nurlu, some three miles behind the line. The book begins at this point.

One

'What kind of a war is it?' was one of the first questions I asked Jack.

'Oh, pretty good,' he replied. 'The guns are five thousand yards from the line, the men spend all their time playing football, you can ride up to the O.P.'

Football at the guns! Horses at the Observation Post! I remembered Ypres last year.

'I don't ride there myself,' he was saying. 'I always feel safer on my own feet. Mind you, there's a lot of breeze,' he added presently.

'What about?' I asked.

'They think Fritz is going to make a big attack, and that it will be on our front.'

'When?'

'Oh, any day now. You've come back just in time for it.'

While I was in hospital I had heard some talk of a forth-coming German attack, but had paid no attention. I supposed that people at the back might always be more nervous than we were. It seemed to me most unlikely that the Germans were going to attack. It might be an agreeable change if they did, we had done all the attacking in 1917. One failure after another. Now the Germans could have their turn.

'It doesn't seem likely,' I said.

'Oh, I don't know about that,' Jack replied. 'And of course we shall get it in the neck if he does come over.'

Jack was always gloomy. He was so pessimistic that he made the rest of us laugh; he cheered us up, we felt certain that nothing would ever be as bad as Jack expected. At any rate there was no sign of an attack at present. Jack himself had said how quiet it was, and I could hear for myself. At Ypres last year we had bombarded the enemy for weeks before our attack, but this morning there was hardly a sound of gunfire, it was more peaceful than anything I had known.

Hardly more than nine months had passed since I joined the battery, a boy almost straight from school, but because the greater part of that time had been spent at Ypres and Passchendaele I already considered myself a veteran. Ypres had been all shells and shell-holes, mud and desolation, but here there was grass, and men played football only three miles from the line.

For the last six weeks I had been away from the battery, first in hospital, then at a convalescent camp. Six weeks was such a long time that I had lost touch with all my friends, and now I felt like a stranger in my own home. No one was expecting me.

Jack had mistaken me for his servant when he saw a figure in the doorway of the hut. 'You can bring me my breakfast now,' he called out. Then he looked up and his smile of welcome convinced me that I was glad to be back. I had been wondering whether I should feel glad to see my friends again or depressed to be at the War again.

'We all thought you were never coming back,' he said.

He told me the battery news while he ate his breakfast. The Major had gone home. 'He fell off his horse in a race and was kicked on the knee,' Jack said. 'There didn't seem much the matter with him, but he went on leave a day or two later, and the next thing we heard was that he was in hospital with a broken knee-cap. What with the war and all the whisky he drank, my own opinion is that he'd had as much as he could stand.'

I was sorry and said so.

'Oh, he was drinking all day and playing hell every night,' Jack said. 'You don't know what he was like at the end.'

I could guess. But he had helped me at the beginning when I felt lonely and lost. Before I came to C Battery I had spent a month in an ammunition column, which must have been one of the worst units in the army. I had been miserable. But C Battery was a different world, and Major Eric, easy-going, ironical, tolerant (when he was sober), and amused by my innocence, had been nice to me and I felt grateful to him, whatever he had been like at the end.

Besides, I disliked changes. Now we should have to adapt ourselves to the ways of some other commander. Major Eric had been very popular with the men. Like themselves he was a Yorkshireman, a Sheffield man, they had known him before they joined up, they thought it right for him to command them. 'He's our mascot, the Major is,' old Driver Oaks had once said to me, 'we don't need no black cat when he's with us.' Now he had gone, and for a moment, in spite of the sunshine outside, I felt a foreboding of misfortune.

'Is Jamieson commanding us then?' I asked.

'For the moment,' Jack said. 'But there's somebody else coming. A fellow called Bingley. He seems to have influential relatives, so the Colonel is keen to have him. But Jamieson is as sick as hell, he thought he was going to command the battery.'

I liked Jamieson. He was a big Australian who had been promoted and come from one of the other batteries in the brigade to be our second-in-command shortly before I went away, but I knew he was not liked by everyone. Frank disliked him, he had been hoping for the promotion himself.

'Where's Frank?' I asked. As senior subaltern in the battery he should have been in charge of the wagon lines, not Jack.

'On leave. And I'm due to go when he comes back. *If* he comes back,' he added gloomily.

'Why shouldn't he come back?'

'I never expect anyone to come back when he goes on leave. Not at the right time anyway. Look at the Major.'

'Is Frank getting married?'

'Not this time, next time he says. It's been next time ever since I knew him. I'm beginning to wonder if he ever will get married.'

But I knew Frank's girl was still at college, she was taking her Finals in the summer.

'He's as sick as hell about Jamieson being promoted before him. He says he was commissioned before Jamieson and has been out here longer.'

Frank as sick as hell about Jamieson, and Jamieson as sick as hell about Bingley. It seemed silly.

3

Jack agreed that it was. 'Can't think why Frankie wants to be a captain,' he said. 'It's more responsibility. I sometimes think I was better off in the ranks. Officers have a more comfortable time, but you stand a better chance of surviving in the ranks.'

Then he asked me about myself. 'Couldn't you have worked things?' he said.

'Not with tonsils,' I replied.

'I'd have had a damned good try, you look pale enough to have got home.'

'I always look pale,' I said, 'but there wasn't much the matter with me.'

'I'm so bloody healthy,' Jack said. 'That's my trouble.'

When he had finished breakfast we went out into the March sunshine and walked round the horse lines. I thought the men looked pleased to see me back, most of them smiled at me. I was not a Yorkshireman, but they had accepted me and they knew I was proud of belonging to their battery. Young Corporal Albert hoped I was feeling champion again. 'I've had no one to sign my letters, Sir,' he said. He knew I would always put my signature on envelopes addressed to his girl without looking inside. I liked Corporal Albert, he was always ready with a smile or a friendly remark, and I could understand what he said; the voices of some of the older Yorkshiremen were almost unintelligible to me.

Then I spoke to Edric, my groom. 'Lady will be glad you're back,' he said. 'She needs more exercise, she's too fat.' He would call my mare Lady, I wanted to change her name to Peggy, but Edric quietly ignored my wishes. He thought a horse had as much right to her name as a man or woman. Walkenshaw, my servant, had been with me while I was away from the battery. He was glad to be back, I saw him talking to his friends and wondered what he was telling them about our time behind the front.

After lunch we rode up to the gun line.

When the battery was in action it was always split into two parts. There was the gun line, where the guns were, usually about two miles behind the infantry in our front line; and there were the wagon lines, where the limbers for moving the guns were kept, and the ammunition wagons, and all the horses, two or three miles further back, out of range of most enemy guns.

The battery commander, generally a major, lived in the gun line; his second-in-command, a captain, at the wagon lines. The four or five subalterns were sometimes in one place, sometimes in the other. They took it in turns to come down to the wagon lines for a rest. So did the gunners. The drivers were always at the wagon lines with their horses, though they took ammunition up to the guns and drove up with the gun limbers before a move. Every gunner and every driver had his special position and responsibility in the battery, changeable only when casualties made change necessary.

The signallers, an elite in the battery, lived in the gun line. On them depended all our communications. The other specialists, shoeing smiths and veterinary sergeant, battery clerk, stores men lived at the wagon lines. The officers' servants went wherever their officers were. There were cooks in both places.

Our 18-pounder guns only had a range of six thousand yards. We could shell the enemy front line and fire at targets immediately behind it, but could not reach anything further back. More distant targets were engaged by the 60-pounders and six-inch howitzers.

The guns were in a long hollow of the downs, between two ridges. The men were not playing football, but were lying about in the sunshine and looked very content. Jamieson gave me a friendly greeting. He had two officers up with him: Hughes had joined the battery shortly before I went away, but this was the first time I had seen Durham. Hughes had been a Welsh policeman before the War; he had enlisted and risen to the rank of sergeant in France before going home to take a commission. Durham also had been in the ranks and in France before he was commissioned, he was hardly older than myself. I liked the look of him, he had red cheeks and a gay smiling face. I felt sure I should have more in common with him than with Hughes, but I already felt a considerable respect for Hughes.

I went to talk to some of the men in my section. There were six guns in an 18-pounder battery, and I was in command of the Left Section, Numbers 5 and 6 guns.

'You've had a long holiday, Sir,' Sergeant Denmark said in his rough disapproving voice. Once I had been afraid of Denmark, he was so gruff and I thought he hardly troubled to conceal his scorn of my ignorance and immaturity. But by this time I hoped I had risen in his esteem and I had learnt that only his manner was unfriendly. He was without fear, and the best sergeant in the battery, I knew that I could depend on him in any crisis. He never had a great deal to say to me, or to anyone else, and he never brought me letters to sign. So far as I knew he did not write any. But he told me now that he was sweating on a leave, he was high on the list and hoping to go within the next few days. Sergeant Denmark was one of the older men in the battery. Most were in their early or middle twenties; some, like Denmark, were over thirty; a few were forty. These were the battery old men, we had to take care of them.

Jamieson was going up to the O.P. and he took me with him. We rode through Heudecourt, a shattered village on the top of the ridge in front of the gun line, and then past the three other batteries in our brigade, A, B and D. They were all nearer to the line than we were, but two of our guns were still further forward, and some way to our right. They were in charge of another new officer, called Griffith, whom I had not yet seen. 'You'll see him soon enough,' Jamieson said.

A and B were 18-pounders, like ourselves, but D was a Four-Point-Five howitzer battery.

The strength of the brigade was about thirty officers and a thousand other ranks and the same number of horses.

I knew all the thirty and was on terms of personal friendship with all except a few of the most senior ones. But with those in the other batteries there could not be the same intimacy there was in our own. We were like brothers, sleeping side by side, within touching distance, sharing whatever possessions we had and the contents of any parcel that came for us.

We did not ride all the way. We left our horses below the last hill, then walked over the crest and down the other side to the O.P., which was in a railway cutting. From the crest of Chapel Hill there was a wonderful view, back as far as Nurlu, where our wagon lines were, and forward for a long way over

6

enemy-held territory. At Ypres it had been difficult to see anything from our O.P.s; I had never seen a living German soldier, except prisoners. Now I saw some, and it gave me a strange feeling. They were our enemies. They had to try and kill us, and we had to try and kill them, but they looked like ourselves and were doing ordinary things. I saw a party of men digging, and two others came out of a red-cross post, I saw the flag fluttering in the breeze. They were a long way off, nearly two miles from us, but they were Germans, they were our enemies.

No one was trying to kill anyone on this warm sunny afternoon. We could not have fired at the men I saw, they were beyond the range of our guns; but none of our longer-range guns was firing, and the enemy had not fired at us as we came over the crest of Chapel Hill and walked down to the railway line. The front line was as peaceful as Salisbury Plain.

Jamieson told me the names of the places we could see— two villages, some copses, the ruins of a sugar beet factory, ridges and ravines. I asked him what he thought about the likelihood of a great German attack, but he was non-committal. 'He may think it's his last chance of winning before the Yanks are ready,' he said; but that was all he would say. He said nothing about Bingley, and I did not tell him what Jack had told me. Bingley might never come. In war nothing was certain until it happened.

I did not stay up with the guns. Jamieson said there was no room for another officer. Indeed one was enough at present, he said, so Hughes rode back to the wagon lines with me in the evening. We raced each other along the downland way, it was perfect galloping country. 'More like a Sunday School treat than a war,' Hughes said as we were riding into camp.

There was nothing for us to do. I went joy-riding every day, galloping over the empty unspoilt country, sometimes alone, more often with Hughes or Durham, chasing the hares, putting up the partridges. After Ypres it was lovely to be in country like this. At Ypres we could not ride at all because of the mud and the shellholes, and when we went further back the country was cultivated and some of the Flemish farmers tried to stop us riding over their land. Here there were no civilians at all. This part of France had been given up by the

Germans in a voluntary withdrawal after the Battle of the Somme, a year before. They had destroyed the houses and cut down the fruit trees before they went, but the country was unspoilt. There were no civilians for ten miles behind us, and not many soldiers—only the divisions holding the line. This was another reason why I did not believe the enemy was going to attack us. If our generals really thought they were, then the back areas would have been full of our reserves. But we saw no one, we had the place to ourselves.

But there was a great deal of talk about a German attack in our Orders, Jack had not exaggerated.

'Where are all these rear defence lines, green and purple and red?' I asked one day. 'I've seen no sign of them.'

'They only exist on paper,' Frank said.

We both laughed, but I did not think it mattered. Even if there was an attack we should hold the enemy, we should never be driven back as far as Nurlu; or only after a long time. The Scottish Division in front of us was very good, the enemy would not get past.

Ours was an Army Brigade of Field Artillery, we were moved from one division to another, according to where we were needed. We were a composite brigade, C Battery was the only Yorkshire one, the men in the other batteries came from Lancashire, and Colonel Richardson, the brigade commander, himself a Lancashire man, was considered by some to favour the other three. As a loyal member of C Battery, but not a Yorkshireman, I thought I could be an impartial judge and I had never noticed any favouritism, but Frank said we were put in the worst position every time.

Frank had returned from leave, and a day or two later Captain Bingley arrived and took over the command of the battery. He seemed likeable. He was elderly, and old-fashioned in his ideas, but he left us alone. Jamieson said he was no good, but we had known he would say so before he saw him. Jamieson in fact had behaved badly. He came down to the wagon lines and said quite frankly to the rest of us that he had handed over to Bingley without telling him all that he needed to know. 'He can find out the rest for himself if he wants to know,' he said.

And as though it was not enough to have two captains in

our battery who were not on speaking terms, there was also this antipathy between Frank and Jamieson. I hoped that leave in England and the company of the girl he loved would have helped Frank to forget his disappointment over promotion, and that he and Jamieson would now settle down and work together, but he was more bitter than ever. 'If Bingley makes a mess of things,' he said, 'it will be Jamieson's fault. He had no right to clear off to the wagon lines so soon, he ought to have stayed up for a couple of days until Bingley had found his feet and knew what we were doing."

I was not worrying at the thought of a German attack, but I did worry about these dissensions in the battery. I loved the battery and had once thought it was the best in France, but it did not seem so good now. I heard less laughter and singing as I walked about the lines and there was more bad temper. It would be strange, I thought, if we could survive Passchendaele and all our casualties and then go to pieces at a time when there was no fighting at all. Even Jack commented on the state of affairs. 'If they go on in this way,' he said, 'I shall wish the Major back.'

He was going on leave, now that Frank had returned, but he seemed more than usually depressed.

'I shan't get very far,' he said. 'They'll cancel all leave and recall everyone as soon as the German Offensive starts."

'Cheer up!' I said, pouring him another whisky. 'You'll miss the first day anyway, and that will be the worst.' I was mocking him, I did not believe these stories of a German Offensive, but his mind was still running on it.

'You know,' he said, 'I always wonder when I go on leave who I shall find here when I get back.'

'We'll take care of ourselves,' I said. 'Don't worry.'

Durham also went on leave. Leave warrants were coming round more quickly than ever before, at the present rate I should be due for another myself by the end of the month. Now there were only four subalterns left, Frank, Hughes, and myself with Bingley in the gun line, and Griffith at the forward section, leaving Jamieson by himself at the wagon lines.

Life was as easy and as comfortable in the gun line as it had been at the wagon lines, and there was not much more to do. I liked Bingley as a man, but as a battery commander he did not inspire confidence. He fussed about trivialities, but appeared to be unaware of what mattered most in a battery, or any other unit—the spirit of comradeship. Frank said he would be all right when he had settled down, and anyway he was better than Jamieson. But even Frank could see the absurdity of some of his behaviour. He was taking the talk of a great German attack very seriously and every night he slept with a loaded revolver by his side.

'Got to be careful if you go into his dug-out before he's properly awake,' Hughes said. 'He may think you're a Fritz.'

'You've nothing to worry about,' Frank told him. 'He won't shoot you, it's to shoot himself, he's terrified of being taken prisoner.'

He was absurd. How could the enemy break through and overrun us before we knew what was happening?

He was one-quarter Irish, he told us; and four-quarters aristocratic birth, his conversation implied. But none of us was interested in hearing about his cousins. He accepted me because I happened to have been at school with a young nephew of his, but Hughes had not been at any school, not what Bingley called a school, and was not accepted by him. Hearing that my father was an Ulsterman, though it was Southern Ireland that he knew, Bingley said we would have a party on the evening of March 17th, to celebrate Saint Patrick's Day, and he invited Major Villiers of A Battery and one of his subalterns.

The weather was perfect. Bingley had been sitting in the sunshine for most of the day in a green canvas chair that he had brought with him from England, with his eyes half closed, listening to the cries of the men who were playing football at the upper end of the valley. 'This is the life,' he said. 'There's nothing like this in England now, England's a depressing place in war-time.''

But his anxiety returned after dinner when the night's orders were brought in. There was more in them about the great German attack, it was expected tomorrow, an under-officer had been taken prisoner and had given information that all the storm-troops were now in readiness behind the line. Bingley followed me outside when I was going to bed. 'We've got to be on the *qui vive* all the time,' he said. 'I've told Hughes to go up to the crest in front before dawn, and I want you to see that he goes.'

I was dismayed at being told to spy on one of my friends, and though Bingley had only been with us for a week that should have been time enough for him to learn that Hughes was completely reliable.

'These ranker officers are all the same,' Bingley was saying. 'Some of them are good up to a point, but you can't depend on them.'

Hughes went up to the crest in the morning. Went and came back again. There was no attack. 'Quiet as a nun's wedding night,' he said at breakfast in answer to our question. There was another alarm the next night. This time it was our aeroplanes, which had seen all the roads behind his line packed with German transport moving up. I was going to believe in the Great Attack when it happened.

Then the weather broke. Thirty-six hours of drizzling rain frayed all our tempers, we always felt irritated when every dug-out became full of wet coats and muddy boots. But after tea the rain stopped and we had an enjoyable argumentative evening. I was late going to my little shelter in the bank, each of us had our own, and I sat there for some time longer, reading and writing up my diary. Writing up my diary and bringing it up to date always gave me a sense of fulfilment, a feeling that now I was ready for whatever was going to happen next.

Two

I seemed to have hardly fallen asleep when I heard someone speaking my name. It was Thirsk, the signaller sergeant. He had raised the gas-curtain over the entrance to my shelter and was shining his torch in my direction.

'Captain's orders, Sir,' he said. 'He wants you to go up to the top of the hill.'

'Now?' I asked irritably. 'In the middle of the night?'

'Yes, Sir. It's four o'clock, Sir. To keep a good look out and send back information.'

Oh, blast the Captain, I thought, blast his nervousness. Well, I reflected it would be light in an hour or two, then I would come back and finish my sleep, I could stay in bed all morning if I liked.

Sergeant Thirsk had gone away. Dressing took some time, for I was in pyjamas, I always undressed completely when the war was quiet.

Sergeant Thirsk came back. 'Sir, he wants you to go quickly,' he said in his soft and unhurried voice. Thirsk was one of the best non-commissioned-officers in the battery, and one of the nicest men. I had never heard him raise his voice or speak angrily, but his signallers were so well trained and so devoted to him that they knew what to do before they were told.

'Any noise outside?' I asked him.

'No, Sir. Only mist.'

At last I was dressed. I put on my soft hat. No need to wear a steel helmet in a war like this. Two signallers were waiting for me outside, and we were about to set off when for the first time I became aware of the sound of gunfire up the line. That was nothing unusual in the hour before dawn, but

12

this morning it seemed heavier than usual. Telling the signallers to wait I went back to my shelter, changed the soft hat for a helmet, and pulled my gas mask round to the alert position in front. Now I was ready for anything.

We began walking up the hill. Thirsk had been right about the fog, it was very thick. But there was a telephone line running along the ground up to our forward section, and I held this in my hand to guide me. Every minute I was expecting the noise in front to die away, this was the usual procedure, but instead of becoming less it seemed to intensify, and now it was not all in front, some shells were passing overhead and falling behind us, and one or two burst at no great distance from ourselves. I began to feel uneasy. We had reached the top of the hill by this time, but the fog was thicker than ever and though day was breaking I could not see more than five yards in front of me.

Then we came to a break in the telephone wire, it had been cut by one of the shells, and because of the fog we could not find the other end. The line had also been broken behind us, I was no longer in communication with anyone, I was stuck at the top of the hill, unable to see more than five yards in any direction. The fog was cold as well as wet, and it was shutting out something else besides the view, it was preventing my finding out what was happening. I felt alone and lost. I certainly should lose my way if I went on, but I could not go back until I had obtained some information. All three of us searched the ground for the other end of the wire, but without success.

The fury of the guns had increased. Now there was gas as well as high explosive. I could not see where any of the shells were bursting, but I could hear the gas shells, they made a different sound when they burst, and I could smell the sickly mustard gas mixing with the clammy smell of the fog.

Something *was* happening up in front and I did not know what it was. I began to feel afraid. It was not the ordinary fear of shells. That was nothing, that stopped as soon as the shelling stopped. This was a new fear and it was not going to stop, it lasted for more than four months, it was the fear of the unknown. A line of infantry came out of the fog, brushing past us on their way up to the line, each man touching the man in front, so as not to lose him. I hoped that one of their officers might have something to tell me, but they knew nothing. They had been in reserve, they had been ordered up—that was all they could tell me. The gas became worse, we had to put on our masks, now it was impossible even to try to look for the other end of the wire. I kept on taking off my mask to smell whether the air was clear, and putting it on again. Sometimes the fog seemed to clear a little then it came down again as thick as before.

In one of these clearer intervals, clear of fog and gas, my signallers found the other end of the wire, and now the line had been mended behind us also, we were in communication with the battery again. I spoke to Bingley, I had no information to give him and he had none for me, but he told me to go on to the forward section, where Griffith was. My signallers told me that Sergeant Thirsk had been badly wounded while out mending the line between ourselves and the guns. I was sorry about this. Thirsk wounded and Denmark at home on leave, they were two of the pillars of the battery, our loss of them was certain, nothing else was certain yet.

I found Griffith eating his breakfast. He was a little Welshman, rather unattractive in appearance, and we had not found any qualities in him to make up for this. Jamieson had sent him up to the forward section to get rid of him, and Bingley had left him there. But he did not appear to mind, and on this worrying morning I was impressed by his unconcern.

'What's happening?' I asked.

He looked at me solemnly while he went on munching. 'Truth to tell,' he said at last, 'I don't know.' He had opened fire with his two guns when the bombardment started, but as nothing seemed to be happening he had stopped. They had suffered no casualties. 'You can't see a thing outside,' he said, as though not knowing that I had been out in the fog for five hours. Hearing that I'd had no breakfast he offered to get me some, but I was not hungry, I ate a slice of bread and marmalade while we were talking and drank some tea.

It was half past nine. I went outside by myself and wondered what I ought to do. It was quieter now, the gunfire on both sides had almost stopped. I heard some machine-gun fire, but not close at hand. Whatever it was that had been

14

happening up in the line seemed to be over now. It was reasonable to suppose that the attack, if there had been an attack, had been repulsed. There might be another, later in the day, but for the moment the situation was under control. I began to think I had been unnecessarily alarmed.

At that moment some figures came running towards me out of the fog. They were on top of me almost before I had seen them. Germans? Of course not. What an absurd idea! But why were they running?

'Jerry's through,' one of them said. He was bewildered, frightened, out of breath from running.

'What's happened?' I asked.

'Jerry's through,' he said again. 'He's in Epehy, we've got no officers left.'

The fog had already swallowed the other men with him, and in a moment he also had disappeared.

I went very quickly back to my signallers and spoke to Frank on the telephone. He put me through to Cherry, the adjutant, at Brigade Headquarters, and I told him what the man had said to me, but he did not accept the truth of the story, it was in contradiction to all the rest of his information, he said. Everyone liked Cherry, but he was too optimistic, he always believed good reports and disbelieved bad ones. So now when he told me that the enemy attack on our front had been repulsed, I did not know whether this was a fact or if it was only what he wanted to believe. Epehy was about a mile in front of where I was and part of our main line of defence. 'These men that you saw,' Cherry said, 'I expect a shell had burst in the middle of their trench and they panicked,' but he told me to keep a sharp look-out, and to let him know at once if I saw anything of the enemy.

I went back to my place. No other figures came running out of the fog. The fog itself disappeared, and the hills and valleys lay bathed in bright sunshine for the rest of the day, the bare sides of Chapel Hill on my left and in front of me, another railway line below me, coming up from behind and running east towards the enemy, and Epehy out of sight, just over the crest on my immediate front. 'Keep a sharp look-out,' Cherry had said. I looked and looked, but there was nothing to see. No German soldiers, no British ones, only the sunlight on the

15

bare hillsides. Was there a battle being fought? I could see nothing of it. Everything looked the same as on any other day.

The hours crawled by. Sometimes I was alone, sometimes Griffith came out to talk to me, or I went to talk to him in his little shelter. He was not a lively companion, but I was glad not to be alone on a day like this. Frank rang up from the battery, 'Keep a sharp look-out on the railway line,' he said, 'there's a report that the enemy is advancing along it." I ran out to my place and searched the line through my glasses. I could see nothing, there was no one there, no one on the part of the line that I could see, only the lengthening shadows creeping across the track.

'I can't see anyone,' I said to Frank.

'No, the report's been denied now,' he said.

At dusk I returned to the battery, and as soon as it was dark the two forward guns were brought back to the main position, it was too risky to leave them for another night. I was hoping to find that I should laugh again when I was in the company of the others, but Hughes was away, he had been sent up as liaison officer at Infantry Battalion Headquarters, and Frank was as worried as I was. Bingley was in a terrible state, he told me. 'I've had to hold his hand all day,' he said.

Only Griffith was in the mood for talking that night. 'Well, I was ready for that,' he said when we had finished dinner. He was always ready for his meals and usually said so. He made a few trite remarks, but none of us were paying any attention to him, and presently I saw that he was writing in his diary.

'I see that it's the first day of spring,' he remarked, 'and in some ways it has been a real spring-like day, hasn't it?'

'Oh, for God's sake, stop talking,' Bingley said.

I went to bed, but tired though I was I could not sleep. Cherry's last report on the situation was that on our front we had not lost a yard of our battle position, only some unimportant outposts. But on our right the situation was obscure, he said; and that amounted to admitting we had been driven back. Frank said that so far as he could gather we had no reserves and that if the Boche attacked again in the morning in the same strength we should not be able to hold him. This

16

was the fear which was keeping me awake; if he attacked again in the morning!

I tried to persuade myself that he must be too tired to do so, remembering how exhausted we had always been at Ypres on the night after one of our attacks. I fell into a troubled sleep at last, but was woken before daylight, woken by the bombardment of German guns, there was nothing tired about them, they sounded terrifyingly fresh. Again there was thick fog, again there was no news. Bingley did not send any of us up to the top of the hill, he seemed incapable of any action. 'O my God!' he said as he came into the mess, 'I can't stand another day like yesterday.'

The fog rolled away and the bad news began to come in. At first it was all from the right. Even Cherry was depressed. He said it was difficult to sort out the conflicting reports but there was no doubt that the enemy had penetrated our battle line at some points.

'O my God!' said Bingley.

Then we heard that one of the divisions on our right had lost the whole of its battle line.

'O my God!' said Bingley.

Then it was Roisel, the enemy was in Roisel.

'O my God!' said Bingley. 'It will be another Sedan.'

I went to sit beside Frank, who had the map in front of him. He pointed to Roisel, due south of us, five miles away. It meant the enemy was half way to Peronne already, and that we were in some danger of having our retreat cut off.

'We ought to be doing something,' Frank said. 'Why aren't we firing?'

One reason was that we did not know the position of the enemy or where our own men were, all the telephone lines in front were broken. Hughes could have told us what the position was, he ought to have returned by this time, he would know where the enemy was, but nothing had been heard of him since the previous night.

'At any rate we could fire on our old S.O.S. lines,' Frank said. Every gun had a line on which it was to open fire in the event of enemy attack. But Bingley said we must conserve our ammunition, we should need it later on.

Cherry rang up again. This time he had information about

our own front: Chapel Hill had been lost, Chapel Hill, our battle line, our main line of defence.

Still Bingley did nothing. 'We must wait for the Colonel's orders,' he said, 'he will tell us what to do." It was a great mistake, he said, to act on one's own initiative, one always found out afterwards that one had done the worst possible thing.

He could not sit still. He kept on getting up and going outside and walking to the end of the line of guns. Then he would come back into the mess and sit down for two or three minutes before going off again. Shells were falling outside, but he was not afraid of shellfire, it was responsibility that he feared, or losing his guns, or being taken prisoner.

'We ought to be doing something,' Frank said again, while Bingley was outside. 'It's absurd to talk about conserving ammunition, we can get more.'

He tried to get through to Brigade Headquarters on his own authority, but there was no answer, they were on the move. The other batteries were already moving back, they had been in front of us, on the far side of the village of Heudecourt, now they were moving into the valley behind us, where we were to join them later in the day.

'I've a good mind to go out myself and see if I can find out what's happening,' Frank said. He was continually taking off his spectacles and polishing the glass with his handkerchief, then rubbing his eyes with his knuckles before he put them back. I could see he was very worried.

But Bingley said there was no need for him to go, and anyway he could not spare him at present. 'We must wait for the Colonel's orders,' he said. The important thing now was to be ready to move back when the order came, it might come at any moment, and we should be in a regular pickle if we were all over the place when it did come, we could do all the firing we wanted after we had moved back.

At three o'clock Hughes returned in a very bad temper. 'Bloody Brigade forgot all about me,' he said. 'Never sent anyone to relieve me, I might have been a bloody stiff by this time for all they care.'

His bad temper was not on his own account, it was because he was desperately worried.

18

'Talk about stiffs!' he said. 'Never seen so many in all my born days.'

'Ours or theirs?' I asked, but I knew what his answer would be before he spoke.

'Ours, every man jack of them, Jocks and South Africans. Jerry brought up his trench mortars in the fog and smashed our trenches to bloody bits.'

'What's happening now?' Frank asked.

'God knows! They were expecting Jerry where I was in ten minutes. They told me to clear out. "Give me a rifle and I'll stay," I said. But they said it wasn't my job to stay and be killed with them.'

'How long ago was that?' Frank asked.

Hughes looked at his watch. 'Half an hour,' he said. 'Jerry will be there now.'

'O my God!' said Bingley. He tried to ring through to Brigade, but there was still no answer.

Then he went outside again and this time Frank followed him. Presently Frank returned by himself. 'I hope you don't mind,' he said to me, 'but I've asked Bingley and he's told me to send you up to the top of the hill. I would have gone myself, but you see what he's like, I have to hold his hand all the time. You'll have to lay out a line as you go. Be quick, and for Christ's sake try to find out what's happening.'

I did not mind going. It was really a relief to have something definite to do, for the first time that day. I set off at once, with two signallers, unrolling the wire as we went. It was fairly quiet, there was some firing in front, not a great deal. Again the sun was shining out of a cloudless sky. If there is anything to see, I thought, I shall see it today. But I knew that things had a way of happening out of sight.

I looked at my watch, it was half past three. We came up to the crest and went on a little way, passing the village of Heudecourt on our left. We went about a thousand yards from the battery, I could not go any further, there was not enough telephone wire. Anyway, there was a good view from here. I could not see into the bottom of the hill below me, that was dead ground from where we were, but I could see all the far side up to the crest of Chapel Hill.

I lay down on the ground and got out my field glasses, I

put them up to my eyes, resting on my elbows. And immediately I saw them. Germans. Thousands of them. Pouring down the side of Chapel Hill. It was the chance of a lifetime. Never before had I seen Germans to shoot at.

'BATTERY ACTION!' I yelled to the signaller behind me.

I pulled out my map and opened it and quickly began to work out the range and angle of fire. Quick, quick! The Germans were coming down the hill in waves and in short rushes. They ran for about a hundred yards, then dropped down for a minute or two, then came on again. My excitement made me slow. Frank will work it out for me, I thought, if I tell him exactly where they are. He was very quick and accurate at map work. I told my signaller to ask him to come to the telephone quickly, but before he could do so there was a message from Bingley: 'Captain says we can't fire,' my signaller said, 'Guns are all packed up ready to move.'

I rushed to the telephone myself. 'THE BOCHE WILL BE HERE IN TEN MINUTES,' I screamed. I was going to add 'unless we stop him,' but as I paused for breath I heard the calm voice of Signaller Burton at the other end repeating my message to Bingley, who must have been standing near the telephone pit. 'Mr Campbell says the Boche will be here in ten minutes, Sir,' I heard him say. He made it sound as though we had invited them to tea and they had rung up to say they would be a few minutes late.

Bingley himself came running to the telephone. 'What's this,' what's this?' he said. 'Germans here in ten minutes! What do you mean, ten minutes? You must be mistaken. We've had no orders, the Colonel would have told me. What do you mean?'

I made a great effort to control myself. It was stupid of me to have exaggerated, the top of Chapel Hill was three thousand yards away, I did not know how long it would take the enemy to come. But in one respect the situation was even more serious than I had at first supposed, my first thought had been that these Germans were attacking our front line, now I realised that our line was somewhere below me, in the ground that I could not see, these Germans coming down the hill were to make the next attack and O God! there might be no one left to resist them.

'There are waves of Germans coming down Chapel Hill,' I said, speaking as calmly as I could. 'We must fire at them.'

'They must be our own men,' he said.

'They're Germans, I can see the shape of their helmets and the colour of their uniforms.'

He did not know what to do. 'The guns are all packed up,' he said. 'I'm expecting the Colonel's order to move back any minute.'

'We must fire,' I said, 'no one else is firing at them.'

'That shows they are our own people.'

'They're Germans, no one else is firing because there's no one left.'

'Are you sure they're Germans?'

'Absolutely certain,' I said.

'Well, you can have two guns,' he said at last. 'But you must be careful with the ammunition.'

Careful with ammunition! For weeks past we had been firing hundreds of rounds every night, without knowing whether we were inflicting a single casualty. Now in broad daylight when I had the whole German Army to shoot at he told me to be careful of ammunition.

I gave my orders to the signaller and waited to see where my ranging shells burst. I had done my calculations very badly, the first two shells fell so far to the right that I almost missed them. I corrected the line. But the next pair burst too high, harmlessly up in the sky. Shrapnel was the right weapon to use against enemy troops in the open, but the shells should burst fifteen feet above them, not a hundred. I corrected the fuse. I had to make three or four corrections before the shells were bursting at the right height, and by the time I had done so the first waves of enemy were out of sight, safely in the dead ground below me. But there were more to come.

All this time we had been under fire ourselves. We might have been seen by an enemy observer, but Heudecourt and the whole of the top of the hill was being shelled, we were not a particular target. A few of the shells fell close to us, one showered earth and chalk on to the map on the ground beside me. I put my arms round my face to protect it, but took no other notice, I was too excited, I kept my eyes on the opposite hillside, waiting for the Germans to appear.

Then I saw them get up and begin to run down the hill. 'FIRE,' I shouted over my shoulder. Ah! that was better, I could see some of the enemy ducking their heads as they heard my shells coming towards them.

'FIVE ROUNDS RAPID!' I shouted.

But there was no report behind me, no shells passed above our heads. What had happened, what had gone wrong? The enemy had escaped me again.

'Captain says we must go in now,' my signaller said. 'Order's come, and we're to go back. He's told guns to stop firing.'

I rushed to the telephone again and asked to speak to Bingley, but he had gone. I tried to speak to Frank, but he was not there. 'Is Mr Hughes there?' I asked. 'No, Sir, he's gone back.'

There was nobody. I gave up. My signallers were looking at me questioningly.

'What are we to do, Sir?'

'We've got to go back,' I said.

We walked down the hill without speaking, the signallers rolling the wire up again as we walked. I was bitterly disappointed with myself. I could pretend that it was all Bingley's fault, but in my heart I knew that I had failed, I was the only person who had *seen* the enemy. If Frank had been in my place he would have ordered the guns to go on firing, whatever Bingley said. So would Hughes. If Bingley had tried to stop them they would have insisted on speaking to Colonel Richardson. That was what I should have done. Asked to be put through to the Colonel. But I had not thought of it. Now it was too late. The chance of a lifetime, and I had thrown it away.

Some weeks later I was awarded the Military Cross. The citation read: He directed the fire of his battery from a most forward position, inflicting heavy casualties on the advancing enemy, exposing himself to great danger and supplying much valuable information throughout.

I was distressed when I read it. It was not true that I had inflicted heavy casualties on the enemy.

Jamieson must have recommended me, he was the only person I had told. Happening to be alone with him a few nights later I told him about the Germans I had seen, and how I had tried to stop their advance, but Bingley would not let me fire. I put all the blame on Bingley when telling the story, but I did not pretend that I had been successful.

I wanted to win the Military Cross, and sometimes as I was falling asleep I had imagined myself doing some brave action. But to win it for something I had not done was distressing, and at first I felt unhappy whenever I caught sight of the purple and white ribbon on my tunic. What would my friends in the battery think if they knew what had really happened! Better to have no medal than to lose their respect. But they said they were pleased and they seemed to think it was all right, my having the medal. If they thought so, then it was all right for me, and I soon became proud of the ribbon. By the time the War came to an end I no longer even felt regret at my failure to kill Germans on Chapel Hill.

Three

Two guns had already left by the time I got back to the battery in the valley and two others were on the point of leaving, but the last two were still in position under the bank, there was no reason why I should not have gone on firing with four guns, or even with all six, for another ten minutes at least. Two wagon loads of ammunition were being taken back with the guns, and Bingley told me to go with them and then to return with the empty wagons for another load. I did not see Frank or any of the others.

We were only going back a thousand yards, into the next downland hollow. We had to go up our valley for a few hundred yards, then turn right, cross over the ridge, and go down into the next valley. The three other batteries in the brigade, A B and D, were there already. There was a horse for me and I rode quickly after the little column, which had just left.

I was still feeling very unhappy because of my failure on the hill. I did not speak to anyone and was not clearly conscious of anything that was happening round me. The wagons were unloaded and in a few minutes I was on my way back with them to the old position. There should have been two limbers as well, for the last two guns, but I had not seen them, I only had the two empty wagons with me, perhaps someone had told me not to wait for them, they would be following. I was riding in front at ordinary walking speed, there was no hurry. I did notice a line of men coming towards me down the side of the hill, they were on my right, they would not actually pass me. I did wonder who they were and what they were doing, but it was not unusual to see a small party of infantry returning from the line.

I was still thinking about the enemy I had seen on Chapel

Hill, not so much about them, I was not wondering where they were now, I was wondering what I ought to have done. But my thoughts were suddenly diverted. I heard a roar of aeroplanes in front, and looking up I saw them coming over the ridge, very low, hardly above tree-top level. Maltese crosses on the underside of their wings! Good God, they were Germans! I had never seen so many. Stop and hope they would not see us? or gallop on? One was coming straight towards us.

'GALLOP,' I shouted over my shoulder.

We flew across the downland, crouching low over our horses. I heard the stuttering of a machine-gun. But in a second or two they were past us, and I could hear my two teams galloping behind me. Over the ridge, down into the hollow, along the bottom, still at the gallop. Then we drew up. One horse slightly wounded in the neck. Good God, what an escape!

Shells had begun to fall round us as we were galloping, we had escaped them also. Everyone on the old position was talking at the same time, everyone was marvelling at his own escape and at ours. I saw another line of men coming down the hill towards us. They would come past us, straight through our position. I went to tell Bingley that I was back. He was not worried about the enemy aeroplanes or the shells, he seemed calmer now than he had been all day. But before I could speak to him an officer came out from the moving line of men and went up to him. 'You'd better clear out,' I heard him say. 'The Boche is in Heudecourt, he'll be here in a few minutes, we were the last to leave.'

For once Bingley made up his mind quickly. There were still two guns on the position, and there were the two wagons with their teams which I had just brought up. In a moment the wagon bodies were unhooked, and their limbers hooked up to the last two guns. In a moment they were galloping up the valley, along the way I had just come. Everything else was abandoned: two wagon bodies, nearly a thousand rounds of ammunition which I might have used against Chapel Hill, maps, orders, telephone wire, stores, everything left behind. I hadn't got a horse, it wasn't my own horse I had been riding, none of us had a horse, we were running straight up the hill,

B   25

that was the shortest way into the next valley. Bingley and myself, the sergeant-major, gunners and signallers. Once I heard myself laughing as we pounded up the hill, it seemed so funny. We were under machine-gun fire, I heard the bullets as we came to the top of the hill, and shells were still falling round us, but the guns were safely over the hill, I could see them in front of us, galloping still.

We could stop running when we were over the crest and going down into the next valley. Edric saw me walking and came to meet me with my horse. But I was puzzled, I was trying to work something out and could not get the answer right. If the Boche was already in Heudecourt, had been there for a quarter of an hour or more, if these lines of retreating infantry were the last men to leave, then why were we here? We had come back a mere thousand yards. If the Boche was already in the valley we had just left, how long would it be before he came to this next one? Had something gone wrong?

I could not think clearly. Too many things had been happening too close together. Possibly I was dreaming, all these events had the absurdity of a dream. I decided to go and find Frank, he would probably have an explanation. But as I was going towards him I heard a curious noise. An explosion of some kind, but not a shell bursting.

'They're blowing up their guns,' someone said.

'Who are blowing up their guns?'

'A and B, they've got no teams up.'

The lines of infantry were passing through us again.

'Time you got out,' an infantryman said. 'No one between us and him.'

I heard two more of the same curious explosions, some little distance away. All the four batteries of our brigade were in line in the valley, A, B, C, D, in that order, A on the right. The curious noises had come from the right.

So it was real, I was not dreaming, A and B were abandoning their guns, and the Boche would be here in a few more minutes. We had six teams up. Six teams and six guns, one for each. They were not the gun teams, but they would do. Everything else would have to be left behind.

'Be quick there,' Frank was shouting.

One of the guns was stuck, it had fallen into a deep shell-hole, the horses could not pull it out. 'We shall have to leave it,' I said. Bombardier Frith dismounted and got into the hole, he put his great shoulders to the wheel of the gun and heaved. The wheel moved a little, but then slipped back. He tried again The other guns were already on the move.

'We must leave it,' I said again. If the other batteries were leaving all their six guns, we could leave one. Bombardier Frith did not speak, his face never moved, he heaved on the wheel with all the great strength of a Yorkshire miner, it was moving, two or three gunners were helping him now, but it was Frith who held the wheel, Frith never let go till the gun was out of the hole. We were the last to leave. Everything else was left behind in the valley, another thousand rounds of ammunition, two or three wagons, all our mess stores, the gramophone and our records, all our personal kit—there were our neatly-rolled valises, lying together where the mess cart had put them down, now the empty mess cart would be half way back to Nurlu, there had been nothing else to carry our valises, and I should have only the clothes I was wearing.

I was riding at the rear of the column, Frank was up at the front with Bingley, I had not seen either Hughes or Griffith since coming down from the hill. We were under machine-gun fire again, but not aimed, there were no enemy in sight. But if they were in the first valley by this time, we might at any moment see them on the crest above us, and then we should come under aimed fire.

For a few hundred yards we were going along the valley, parallel to the line of the enemy's advance, then we turned sharply right, away from him, along the track leading to Nurlu, where our wagon lines had been. It was as we were turning, as the front of our little column was beginning to climb the hill that I had a sudden impulse to go back, I was going back to get the rug out of my valise.

Without a word to anyone I turned round and galloped back along the way we had just come, along the deserted valley, past the ill-fated gun position, back to the pile of neatly-rolled valises lying on the ground where the mess cart had dumped them.

Two men were there. Germans? No, English officers. One was sitting in Bingley's green canvas chair, the other was unrolling one of the valises, my valise. Where on earth had they come from?

'Time you got out,' I shouted. 'The Boche will be here in a few minutes.'

'We're waiting for him,' said the man in the green canvas chair.

I saw they were both padres. 'Most of our men who are left have been taken prisoner,' said the man in the chair, 'our place is with them.' The other man was taking the rug out of my valise.

'I want that,' I said, 'it's what I've come back for.'

'Oh, it's yours, is it?' he said. 'Sorry.'

'Take anything else you like,' I said. But I was pulling things out of the valise, wondering what else I could take. Quick, quick! Any minute now!

The man in the chair had come over to me, he gave me a sheet of paper, torn out of his note book, on which he had written his name and address. 'Write to my wife,' he said.

I took the paper, I shook hands with them both, I grabbed my big writing case, it contained my 1917 diary, the book I was reading, and a letter from a girl. Then back on to my horse, and I was galloping along the valley again, I had been a bit longer than I had intended because of talking to the two chaplains, but I should catch up with the others, probably before they had even noticed my absence.

But at the same corner, at the very place where I had turned back before, I nearly rode into three other men. Scottish machine-gunners. One of them was wounded, the other two were wheeling him along on a bicycle. They had got him down the hill, but it was proving more difficult to push him up on the other side. I dismounted again before I had thought what I was doing. 'We can put him on my horse,' I said. Between us we lifted the wounded man into the saddle. This was another delay, I reflected, the rest of the battery was already over the top of the hill and out of sight; but galloping, I should soon catch them up when the friends of the wounded man had taken him again at the top, it would be easy for them to wheel him on the level.

I was leading my horse, the two men with the bicycle were behind me, but when I looked round at the top of the hill they were not there. Somehow they had got in front of me, they were quite a long way off, they were riding away on the bicycle. I shouted. But they did not hear me, or may not have wanted to, and the sound of my own voice made me realise how alone I was. Alone with a wounded soldier in the middle of a battle! The cyclists were out of sight now. There was no human being in sight. The rest of the battery and the retreating infantry had crossed the plateau and were now hidden from me in lower ground. Somewhere behind us were the Germans. I turned round to look, but they had not yet come over the crest behind me. Our army on one side, the Germans on the other, and between the two myself and my horse and a wounded Scottish machine-gunner on her back.

The battlefield was as silent as it was deserted. The aeroplanes had gone, the shellfire had ceased. The calm evening sunshine lay over the downland, the shadows were beginning to lengthen. It was beautiful. The battlefield was beautiful. I could not see into the hollow where our guns had been, I could only see some of the abandoned guns on the other side of the track. They looked out of place, incongruous with the peaceful scene, one or two were pointing up to the sky at a grotesque angle. But there was nothing else to mar the quiet dignity of the downs, there was nothing else to see, only some deserted guns and a wounded man on a horse.

Well, I had got myself into a proper mess. But there was no way out of it now, I should have to look after my wounded man until I could hand him over to the care of someone more fitted than myself. Fortunately I knew the position of a Field Ambulance on this side of Nurlu. But it would take a full half hour to get there, it would be nearly dark, how on earth could I find the battery in the dark! I knew it was retreating through Nurlu, everything had to go through Nurlu, but I had no idea of its destination on the other side. And what should I say to Frank and Bingley when I did find them! It was a serious matter to go off without orders in the middle of a battle. I did not really think Bingley would want to court-martial me, but I knew that my behaviour could be described as desertion in the face of the enemy.

The man's wound was worse than I had at first supposed. He was in pain, I was afraid of his falling off, I could not have

29

lifted him back by myself. I had to support him in the saddle as well as leading my horse. I put the rug round my shoulders and gave him the writing case to carry, so as to have both hands free. He dropped it on the way, I never saw it again. But I still had the rug.

The sun was only a little way above the horizon, a great red ball in front of me as I walked up the last hill and came to the Field Ambulance. A doctor, a captain in the RAMC; was on the point of driving away in a car. I explained to him what had happened and waited for him to free me of my responsibility. But he said he could not take my soldier, all their wounded had been evacuated, the last ambulance had left.

'You must take him,' I said. 'I can't leave him for the Boche, and I can't go on leading him all over France, I've got to find my battery.'

The doctor looked at me, he looked at the wounded Scotsman, who had taken no part in our conversation, he and I had hardly exchanged a word on our way.

'All right,' he said. 'I'll take him.' He called to someone behind him. Two men came out of a hut, they lifted the man down and carried him away on a stretcher.

At last I was free. Now I must get to the other side of Nurlu as quickly as possible, that was where I must begin looking for the battery. The enemy was shelling Nurlu, there was a cross-roads in the middle of the village, everything had to pass it, guns, wagons, lorries, everything, and the enemy's fire was directed at the cross-roads. Big stuff. It sounded like eight-inch, one shell every two or three minutes. The wagons waited on the road at a safe distance, waited for a shell to burst, then galloped past the danger spot at a mad speed, half a dozen at a time. One too many went. I heard the scream of an approaching shell, followed by a tremendous explosion, and a great cloud of black smoke rose into the air.

I saw what had happened as soon as I turned the corner, dead men and horses lay sprawled across the road. One man was still alive, I saw him struggling to get up, and while I looked I saw another man come out and raise the wounded man in his arms and move him a little, out of the way of other galloping wagons.

It might be one of our wagons that had been hit, I thought,

between us we might be able to hoist another wounded man on to my horse. I rode quickly up to the cross-roads. 'Anything I can do to help?' I asked.

But one look at the face of the wounded man was enough to show me there was nothing I could do, nor anyone else. The man who was holding the dying soldier looked up at me, I saw his black regimental badge, it was another padre. He was kneeling in the most dangerous place in Nurlu, at that moment there may have been no more dangerous place on the whole of the Western Front. I should have to change my opinion of padres, I thought. We did not have one in our brigade, only a doctor, but I had come across several, always behind the line, they had not been impressive. Now it seemed there was another kind of padre.

'Are you a doctor?' he asked. He was kneeling on the road, holding the dying man in his arms, looking up at me.

I shook my head.

'Then go away,' he said. 'In God's name, go quickly.'

But I turned round for a last look as I was riding away. I saw the dead men and the horses lying across the road, no wagons were coming by, another shell was due, I heard it coming, I saw the padre bend low over the man he was holding, but the shell burst a little way off, smoke and brick dust filled the air, but this time it was only a house that had been hit. That was my last sight of Nurlu.

I looked everywhere for the battery. I stood at the side of the road, looking at every gun or wagon that came past me, hoping to see a familiar face. Then leaving the road I went to every place I could see where there were horses, and at one of these I found our wagon lines. Jamieson was there, he had moved back during the afternoon, he told me. He also was looking for the guns; but less zealously, I thought, than I had been. He told me to stay with him and I was glad to do so. It was not my right place, but at any rate I was no longer lost. To my surprise I saw Hughes and Griffith there. I did not ask them how they had become separated from Bingley and Frank, and they asked me no questions. A meal was ready, we sat down on the ground, but before we had begun to eat there was an order for us to move immediately.

Putting some biscuits into my pocket I got back on to my

31

horse, and as I did so I felt that all my strength had gone. Excitement and a sense of responsibility had kept me going through the last four or five hours, from the moment that I had begun walking up the hill towards Heudecourt; now suddenly, as darkness fell, I knew that I was finished, I could do no more.

And as my strength had gone, so had my courage, and instead of wanting to be up in the front of the battle I was eager to go back, to get as far away as possible from the enemy, to go more quickly, not to be held up on the road, the road was packed with other transport, we were stuck, we should never get away. I did not know where we were going, but it seemed only too probable that the enemy would get there first.

Now for the first time a realisation of the magnitude of our defeat came over me and overcame me. This was the most catastrophic defeat that Britain had ever suffered, and it seemed to me that I was partly responsible for the disaster. I could have stopped the enemy on Chapel Hill, I ought to have done so. We had left two thousand rounds of ammunition behind us, if I had kept my head we could have fired them all, we might have killed two thousand Germans. That was my job—to kill Germans, not to go galloping about with a rug or taking a wounded Scottish machine-gunner on my horse.

To left and right of us the blackness of the night sky was lit up with explosions. Petrol stores and ammunition dumps were being blown up, to prevent their falling into the hands of the enemy. Huts were blazing all round us. At one stage of our march I found Corporal Albert riding at my side. 'Some of the lads is saying, Sir, that we're luring Jerry on,' he said to me. 'What do you think, Sir?'

I could see his white anxious unhappy face by the light of the burning huts. He was frightened, he needed re-assurance, he wanted help from me, to be told that it was all right, but I could not help him, I was as unhappy as he was, and more despondent.

'I don't know,' I said. 'I don't know what to think.'

We stopped at last. I did not know where we were. We did not seem to be anywhere. But there were no Germans. It was very cold. Ropes were put up between the wagons, the horses were tied to them, horses and men were given something to eat. 'The servants have got some grub for us,' Hughes said. I followed him into a hut of some kind, there was a roof over our heads and candles were burning, it was a relief to get out of the cold night. Somebody was saying something about eggs. 'At least three hundred,' I heard Hughes say. 'Poor devil had to pack up a second time and leave everything.' That was why we were eating buttered eggs, I supposed; but I hardly knew what I was eating, I was so tired.

I fell asleep lying on the floor. Once I woke up and heard Frank swearing. So he had succeeded in finding us, though we had failed to find him. I heard him saying that none of the men with the guns had any food at all. That was why he was swearing. He would have liked to swear at Jamieson, whose responsibility it was to feed the gun line, but not being able to swear at him he cursed the luckless Griffith instead. Everyone in a bad temper always swore at Griffith. I heard the two of them riding away into the darkness of the night. I felt mean to go on sleeping and lying in the warmth of the hut, but only a direct order could have made me move.

I awoke again an hour or two later, before daybreak. It was the German guns again that woke me, but this time they were more distant, we had retreated a long way. At once I remembered everything, my failure and bitter discouragement. But soon the others began stirring, and I felt better when we began to talk. I was able to enjoy my breakfast eggs. But most of the men had been out in the open all night, some without blankets had had to walk about all the time because they were too cold to lie down.

Bingley and Frank and Griffith arrived with the six guns, and they were given their eggs. 'Hello!' Frank said crossly when he saw me, 'what happened to you? Where did you go off to?' But he was not interested in my answer, it was easy to be evasive. Bingley never noticed I was there, he probably had not noticed my absence either.

Then Colonel Richardson, the Brigade Commander, came with all his Headquarters Staff, and there were eggs for them too. The Colonel said we had nothing to reproach ourselves for, we had fought magnificently, the courage of the whole of the Fifth Army had been beyond praise, we had been outnumbered, five or six to one, but everywhere we had put up the most determined resistance, and the Boche casualties had been simply enormous. I did not believe all that he was saying, but perhaps it had not been such a terrible defeat as I had at first thought.

Cherry said we had nothing to worry about. The French were marching to our assistance at full speed. Two Army Corps, a hundred thousand men at least. We had only to hold on for one more day. I did not believe him either, but perhaps somebody some day would come up from behind to help us.

The Colonel and Cherry rode away. Bingley also went away. He was on the verge of collapse and the Colonel sent him back to get some sleep. Frank went with him. Jamieson stayed up with the guns. It was a relief to have him in command. He was imperturbable, he behaved as though nothing out of the ordinary had happened. Hughes, the Welsh policeman, was equally calm. 'Jerry's turn today,' he said, 'our turn again tomorrow.'

Four

The Retreat went on.

We stayed where we were, in the Frenchman's hut, eating more of his eggs, until afternoon. From a high bank behind the guns I saw an enemy battery driving along the road out of Nurlu, the road where we had been the night before. I hated them. They looked so arrogant, so sure of themselves. Nobody was firing at them, there was nothing we could do, they were far beyond the range of our guns. I watched them driving along the road, then coming down the side of the hill, over the green turf of the downs. I saw them halt, the guns were drawn up in position for firing and the horses taken back over the hill. It was effortlessly done, no one making any attempt to stop them, I might have been watching a ceremonial parade.

This may have been the battery which fired at us during the afternoon. The shells did us no harm. Most of the men were asleep in the sunshine, making up the sleep they had lost. They woke up, looked at the shell bursts, which were a little way from us, and went to sleep again.

And sometime after this we received the order to retreat again. We came to the little town of Combles. There was nothing left of it. Now we were out of the unspoilt country and coming into the devastated area, the old Somme battle-field of 1916. Villages were mounds of rubble, woods were splintered stumps, there were tumbledown trenches on both sides of the road and coils of rusted wire.

We passed through Combles and climbed the hill on the other side. There we stopped. The guns were drawn up in line, ready to open fire if we had to. We went to look for sleeping places for ourselves in the old trenches.

'If we had some rum,' Hughes said, 'we could put it in our tea, if we had any tea.' Presently there was rum and tea for everyone. And a hot meal.

'I was ready for that,' Griffith said.

My own spirits began to rise, we seemed less on our own, there was a battery of 60-pounder guns close to us. I went with Jamieson to talk to some of their officers.

'We shall have to use the *Daily Mail* War Map if we have to fire,' their battery commander told us. 'It's the only one we've got. Our thoughtful Staff has omitted to supply us with maps of the back area.'

'They know the British never retreat,' Jamieson said.

He and I shared a little shelter leading out from one of the old trenches. Though it was less cold there than at ground level I should have been cold with only my one rug, but Jamieson shared his blankets with me, and it was while we were lying side by side in our narrow cell that I told him about the Germans I had seen on Chapel Hill.

Again we were wakened early, this time not by German guns, but by an orderly from Brigade Headquarters with our orders for the day. Sitting up in the trench I read them over Jamieson's shoulder. O God! We were to send out an officer at once with a gun and a hundred rounds of ammunition. To engage the enemy over open sights, to inflict casualties and hold up his advance. It was my turn, Hughes had gone out by himself during the previous afternoon and Griffith had been taken by Frank in the night. But this was something far worse, it was a suicide job, it was asking to be killed.

'Shall I go?' I said. I wanted to be able to pretend that I had volunteered.

Jamieson did not answer at once, and I was aware of a faint spark of hope, for I could see from his face that he agreed with me that it was suicidal, and he was asking himself which of us would be the least loss to the battery. My hope increased, for if I was right I guessed what his answer would be.

'No, I'll send Griffith,' he said.

It was unfair, Griffith was given all the rotten jobs, but I could not have offered again, and I could not help admiring Griffith as he rode away with his gun. He seemed utterly unconcerned, he was only worrying about his breakfast, which there had been no time for.

'They'll give him breakfast in heaven,' Hughes remarked, as we watched them going down the hill.

None of us thought we should ever see him again, or his gun or any of the men with him. For engaging the enemy over open sights meant that he could see you as easily as you could see him, and Griffith and his men would be overwhelmed as soon as they appeared over the skyline, they might be surrounded by enemy infantry at once, they would certainly come under very heavy fire.

Soon we were on the move again ourselves, the retreat was continuing. First I saw our infantry, what was left of them, wearily climbing the hill towards us, and then the enemy coming down the opposite slope into Combles. If that was the way Griffith had gone he might already have been taken prisoner.

Jamieson and Hughes had already left with the guns, I had not yet started, some of our wagons had gone to fill up with ammunition and Jamieson had told me to await their return. They had returned and I was about to set off with them when I saw Hughes galloping towards me.

'Got to go and find Griffith,' he shouted as soon as he was within hearing.

'But he knows he's got to come back on his own,' I said. 'He knows that no one's going out for him. I saw the orders.'

Hughes had seen them too. I tried to persuade him not to go, I thought he was certain to be captured or killed. I pointed to the enemy on the opposite slope.

'Got to obey orders,' he said crossly. He added that it was not Jamieson's fault, it was some crazy idea of Brigade's.

'Where is Jerry?' he said, and I showed him again the enemy I had seen.

'I'll see if I can keep out of their way,' he said, and he turned half right and galloped down the hill.

I was very distressed. Even if he succeeded in avoiding the enemy he did not know where Griffith had gone, he might be anywhere; how could Hughes find him? Griffith might be no great loss, though he had some good men with him, but to lose Hughes as well would be a disaster.

They all returned safely. During the afternoon we found them waiting for us at a cross-roads. Hughes laughed when I asked him what had happened. 'Don't think he gave Jerry much of a headache, between you and me,' he said. Griffith had not gone very far, he had not engaged the enemy over open sights. He had taken his gun behind a hill and had then opened fire without having any idea whether he was hurting the enemy. Before they had fired a dozen rounds the breech jammed, and while Sergeant Tommy Doff was trying to repair it Griffith sat on the ground and began to eat the breakfast he had brought with him. That was where Hughes had found him.

'Can you beat it!' he said. 'Sitting on his arse, eating his grub, and old Jerry on both sides of him.'

I wondered how any of them had escaped, but Hughes said he knew the country well, having fought in those parts in 1916.

All day we were retreating. Guillemont, Trones Wood and Delville Wood, Bernafay Wood, Montauban, Carnoy, Maricourt. Names I had heard for the first time while I was still a boy at school. On this one day we crossed from one side to the other of the old Somme battlefield, giving up in one day what had taken us four months to win.

At Maricourt we turned south, leaving the upland plateau on which we had been since our retreat started, and descending steeply into the valley of the River Somme. There, at a place called Suzanne, and a little before dusk, we stopped. Bingley and Frank were waiting for us at Suzanne. I was hoping that Jamieson would have remained in command for some time longer, but Bingley was a conscientious person and he said he was himself again now, leaving us to wonder what that meant. Whatever it might mean, Bingley was in command of us again now, and Jamieson went back to the wagon lines, which were a little way in the rear.

Unlike the other villages neither Maricourt nor Suzanne was completely destroyed. They had been behind our line when the Battle of the Somme started in 1916. Every house was damaged, but walls were still standing. The battery had halted a little way out of Suzanne, and we found a small deserted army hut in which we could eat and sleep. Orders

38

for the next day arrived as we were finishing our meal. Again we were to send out an officer, but this time he was not to take a gun with him. This time it was a much simpler affair, he was to take two signallers with him, find out where the enemy was, and send back information.

Bingley told me to start at half past four, so as to be up on the hill above the river before daylight.

Five

mid-March

The signaller on duty called me, lighting the candle at my side, saying that my signallers were waiting for me. I had only taken off my tunic, and puttees and boots, and within a few minutes I was ready to go.

We set off in the darkness, walking up hill, away from the river valley, back towards Maricourt and the high ground we had come from on the previous day. It was not a particularly difficult job that I had been given: to find out where the enemy was and send back information. Any infantry officer would have something to tell me about the situation so far as his battalion was concerned, I intended to speak to two or three if I could, then make my own report from what they told me, and send it back to Cherry at Brigade Headquarters. I should have to send one of my signallers, we had no telephone line. But from my point of view this was not something to be regretted. With only two signallers to send back, I should have to return with the third report myself, which might well be the end of my job. By then probably we should be in retreat again.

But though there was no reason to suppose that my task would be unduly difficult, I was feeling very depressed as we started off. Tiredness and the continuous anxiety of the last few days had undermined my confidence and strength. I was afraid, I felt alone, none of the others in the hut had woken when I went out, I should have felt less discouraged if one of them had been awake and had wished me luck before I started. And as for the battle, it seemed as though we should go on retreating for ever, I could see no end to it.

It was not difficult to find the way, there was a track leading in the right direction and enough light to follow it. But no

40

one else was about. We met nobody on our way, the night was quiet, hardly a gun firing. We came to a wood and walked along beside it. Track and wood ended when we came to a road running left and right of us. I could tell we were at the edge of a cliff, the river Somme was below us. Here I would wait until daylight.

I had not long to wait. The valley was hidden in fog, almost up to the level of my eyes, but even as I watched the sun began to break through and the mist to dissolve. The river was two hundred feet below me, an almost sheer drop, and the spectacular sight took my breath away. All the upland country was the same, there was no variety in it, but here was a broad and beautiful valley, the river flowing through lakes and lonely marshland. My first thought was that this was a line we could hold, the enemy could never get across if the cliff was held by a few resolute men; but as soon as I looked at the map I saw that he would not have to get across, the river was flowing east and west, he would come over the uplands, he could turn this position with no difficulty at all.

I stood at the side of the road, in an old trench, looking down into the valley below me. The war seemed to have stopped. The guns were silent, we were alone, there was neither friend nor foe in sight, only the grey ruin of a church by the river, lit by the morning sun, like an old ruined abbey in the middle of a deserted land.

Then to my dismay I saw Major John coming up the hill behind me. He was the commander of our D Battery, the man most disliked and most feared in the whole brigade. Without fear himself he expected others to be equally unafraid; he despised you if you showed fear, and I had been feeling afraid ever since I woke up. I knew he would expect me to go with him on some crazy enterprise, he was always doing crazy things. Though he had often been wounded, he seemed to bear a charmed life.

At Heudecourt, for instance, on the night of the disaster, when A and B Batteries blew up their guns, he had gone forward alone to find out where the enemy was, ordering his battery to stay where they were until he returned. Frank had been telling us about him. 'He thought we had lost the war,' Frank said, 'and his idea was to wait for the Boche and then

41

open fire at point-blank range until they were themselves all killed.'

Of course his battery had not stayed. The infantry had told us that the Boche would be here in a few minutes, what was the point of waiting to be taken prisoner? They had retreated with us, never expecting to see their commander again. But somehow he had escaped capture, and had gone berserk, Frank said, when he returned and found his battery was not there.

This was the man who was now coming up the hill behind me. There was just a chance that he might not know me and might go on by himself; he had never spoken to me, he talked with generals, not with insignificant people like myself. But it was a vain hope, Major John knew everyone.

'What's happening here?' he asked in his unpleasant voice. He had a habit of ending his sentences with a short disagreeable laugh, you could not tell if he meant what he said or if he was mocking you. I told him nothing was happening at present and that I had seen no sign of the enemy. For a minute or two he stood beside me, looking through his field glasses at the country in front of us. I looked through mine, hoping to give an impression that I was doing a useful job.

'No, there's nothing for us to do here,' he said. 'We'll go on to Maricourt and find out what's happening there.'

It was as I had feared. *We'll* go, he had said; go out looking for trouble!

But an extraordinary thing happened. As I walked beside him I no longer felt afraid. I was walking normally, erect, not bending down so as to be nearer the ground. He talked, I listened. He talked to me as an equal, not as a senior officer to a very junior one, not as a high-up Indian Civil Servant, which was what I knew he had been before the War, but as one soldier to another. He talked about the battle we were fighting. He admitted that there had been a moment when he thought that everything was lost. 'No plan of retreat, no reserves, what generalship!' he said.

We ourselves enjoyed criticising the Staff and Higher Command, and it was a satisfaction to hear a senior officer like Major John doing the same thing. His subalterns said that divisional generals came to ask his advice, and they had heard him say to one of them, 'You don't want the War to end because you will go down in rank when it's over, but I shall go up,' referring to his position in India.

We came to Maricourt, which was on the high plateau, a little way back from the river valley. There was an old trench at the edge of the village in which half a dozen infantrymen were standing. They called out to us to get down. Major John looked at them, but did not answer.

'Get down!' they said again. 'You're under observation.'

'I think you're mistaken,' he said.

He deliberately stepped across the trench and stood on a little mound of earth on the German side. He raised himself to his full height and stood there while I might have counted twenty.

'You can see for yourselves,' he said, 'that there are no Germans within a thousand yards of us.'

I did not know what he was going to do next, he was no longer taking any notice of me, and it seemed the right moment to eat one of the sandwiches that my servant had made for me the night before. I offered one to him when he rejoined me.

'I don't see why I should deprive you of your breakfast,' he said. He had brought nothing for himself, and it was in keeping with his character that he should come out to see for himself and, alone, instead of sending one of his officers as Bingley had sent me.

I said I had more than enough for myself. He looked at my packet of sandwiches. 'They look very appetising,' he said. How anyone could use such a word to describe one of Walkenshaw's sandwiches, I did not know. My servant had many good qualities, but sandwich making was not one of them. He cut two thick slices of bread, smeared them with butter, and put a slab of bully beef between them. But Major John was as indifferent to food as he was to danger, he ate only because he was hungry, and he was hungry now.

We were sitting on the top of the trench with our legs dangling inside, opposite each other, and he was talking now about other wars and other generals, Napoleon, Clive, Marlborough. I was able to comment on what he was saying because of my own interest in history, but he may have been talking to himself more than to me. Refusing my offer of another sandwich he got up to go. I wanted to go with him, I would have followed wherever he led me, but he told me that my place was in Maricourt, I was to stay there as long as I could and supply Headquarters with accurate information.

My courage remained high for an hour or more after he had left me. He had not only restored my confidence in myself, he had made me believe that the war was not lost. The Germans had missed their chance, he said; they had not destroyed us, they would find it difficult to move their guns across the devastated area, we should have to go on retreating for another day or two, but our reserves would have time to come up and then the enemy would be stopped.

He had given me back my courage, I no longer wanted to get away from Maricourt. But then a disconcerting thing happened. I was standing in the trench, looking out in front of me, resting my elbows on the parapet, exposing myself more than was necessary in order to see. A foot or two above my head there was an old strand of yellow telephone wire, sagging between two posts. Suddenly the wire snapped, one of the ends fell on to my steel helmet with a little tinny sound, and in the same instant I heard the crack of a rifle in front of me.

The sniper had missed. But the realisation that he had seen me and that his aim had been so nearly accurate was very frightening and I felt my confidence slipping away again. I moved to another part of the trench and now I was very careful when I looked over the edge.

It was the first sign of enemy activity that I had seen, but shells soon began falling on Maricourt, and a little later on my right I saw our outposts falling back. On other days this had been the prelude to the enemy's advance, we had seen our men coming back and then the enemy coming forward, and I assumed that this was about to happen now and that Maricourt would be abandoned. It was time for me to think about my own retreat. I had already sent one of my signallers back, now I sent the other with a written message to Headquarters about the men I had seen coming back.

I stayed in the trench a little longer, waiting for Germans to appear, but now I wanted an excuse to return and I found one when the infantry in my trench got up and started to go back. They told me they had been ordered to retreat, that the enemy was already in one part of Maricourt. I ought to have obtained confirmation of what they said, but it was what I had been expecting and I went to Brigade Headquarters and told Cherry that the Germans were in Maricourt. This was incorrect. Cherry was better informed than myself, because Major John had only just left him and he had found out far more than I had. The Germans had not yet attacked Maricourt, there was no present intention of abandoning it.

Cherry took me outside and from where we stood we could see German shells falling on the village, there was a pall of dark smoke over the houses. That showed it was still in our hands, and I felt ashamed of my inaccurate report. If I had not been so frightened by that sniper's bullet I should have used my eyes and seen for myself that we were still holding Maricourt.

Since it had not fallen my place was there, and I suggested that I should go back. But Colonel Richardson was considerate to his junior officers, and he probably realised that I could take no more for the present. He sent me back to the battery, where I found the others on the point of sitting down to a lunch of hot maconachie stew, and after that and a much stronger drink of whisky than I was in the habit of taking I felt restored. I would not have minded going back to Maricourt, but Bingley had no orders for me.

I was not the only person who had had a bad morning, Hughes told me—Bingley had lost his chocolate. I heard about it from himself during the afternoon. It had been stolen out of his saddle-bag, he always kept it there, for use in an emergency, everyone knew that he kept chocolate there, he had done so in every battery in which he had served, and this was the first time it had ever been taken. Of course he knew what men were, he said, they did take things, but not from their own officers; that was the point; he would not have minded if it had been men from another battery, but no one else could have taken it, he wasn't worrying about the loss of the chocolate, it was the fact that these Territorials had such a poor sense of loyalty that they would steal even from their own officers. That was the mark of a second-rate battery, he said.

45

He had a bad afternoon as well. The sun had gone behind clouds, it looked as though it might rain, and Bingley had lost his mackintosh. It had been left behind at Heudecourt with all the rest of our kit. But getting wet, Bingley told us, always brought on his rheumatism, and if he got an attack of rheumatism he was no more use than a sucked orange, he said. He went outside, looking anxiously up at the dark clouds, and I heard him asking an infantry officer who went by if he happened to have such a thing as a spare mackintosh. He rang up Cherry, telling him of his predicament, and either he or the Colonel found something for him.

I had time to write a short letter to my parents, the first I had written since the battle started, and I gave it to a dispatch rider who was passing by on a motor bicycle. But he lost it or forgot about it, or he may himself have become a casualty. The letter never arrived, and my parents not hearing from me for so long thought I was killed or a prisoner. Frank was reading *The Times* and the first account of the battle that we had seen, the others were sleeping. I heard Frank's short bitter laugh, not a cheerful sound at any time. 'We have fought the enemy to a standstill,' he quoted, 'and I think you'll be glad to know that we're all in our usual high spirits.'

Dusk was descending before we received the order to retreat again, the guns had stayed in the same position for twenty-four hours. Maricourt had not yet fallen, it was still being shelled. I could see the pall of smoke over the village as we moved out on to the road. Major John's battery was still firing when we went past them, he never left any of his ammunition, he always found some enemy to shoot at. I saw him standing behind one of his guns as we went by and he saw me and gave me one of his grim smiles. The look on his face made me think that he knew about my fear after he left me and how I had taken back inaccurate information, and I was disappointed at the thought of having lost his good opinion, which I believed I had won in the morning. But I could not help it, it was impossible to live up to his standards; and even he, I thought, might have been shaken by that sniper's bullet. I could hear the tinny sound on my helmet still.

For hour after hour we marched through the night or were halted on the road, waiting for orders. At first we were in the valley; there was a smell of marsh and mist and I could see the dim shapes of trees by the river. Then we began to climb. Road and hill seemed to go on for ever. At first I heard singing and laughter, but as hour followed hour the men became silent and then there was nothing to hear but the sound of horses' feet on the road, the straining of harness, and the jolting and creaking of wheels.

The night was bitterly cold. I was so cold that I could not ride my horse. I dismounted and walked along the road, leading her behind me. For much of the way Frank was walking at my side. We hardly talked, but there was companionship even in silence.

'Shall we ever get there?' I asked once.

'We shall get somewhere,' he said.

There were French civilians in one of the villages we passed through. We had crossed over the area of devastation, now we were on the other side, in country that had never yet been fought over. Like ourselves, the inhabitants were in retreat. We saw them bringing out their possessions and loading them up on to carts, as much as they would hold, or there was time for.

'Here we are!' I heard someone say at last. The guns and wagons had pulled off the road into a field. Edric came and led my horse away, but I remained standing where I was. I was too tired to move.

'This is the stuff for the troops,' Hughes said, bringing me a mug of tea well laced with rum. I followed him in the darkness along a railway track until we came to a little hut, like a plate-layers', beside the line. Inside the hut there were three beds made of wire netting, with railway carriage cushions for mattresses. Griffith was already asleep on one of them, Hughes and I lay down on the others.

I did not wake up until eleven o'clock. The door of the hut was open, the sun was shining, Hughes was not there. 'Where's Mr Hughes?' I asked Walkenshaw when he brought in my tea. 'Gone out two hours ago,' he said. He told me that the Captain had sent a message for me to go, but Hughes being nearest to the door had woken up when the signaller came in, and he said he would go in my place. 'He said you were pretty near whacked,' Walkenshaw said.

It was a blow to my pride to hear him talking about me in this way, but our servants always discussed us of course. When Hughes returned he did not tell me that he had gone out instead of me and when I thanked him, he said it was nothing, he wasn't tired, he said, he'd had a slack time the day before, I would have done the same for him, he said.

The Retreat went on.

During the night we had retreated nearly to the river Ancre, which flows into the Somme a few miles above Amiens. Bingley sent me to reconnoitre the river crossings, to find out whether the bridges were strong enough to take our guns and whether the Germans were already across the river. I saw an infantry captain by himself among the trees in the valley and decided to ask him for information. We talked for a few minutes, he had not a great deal to tell me, but he said he thought the enemy would not reach the river for at least another half hour.

What a strange war it had become, I was thinking. Here was I sent out to find where the enemy was and no one seemed to know, and here was this infantry officer, alone and distraught-looking, appearing hardly to know where he was or what he was doing. We were in no obvious danger, there was no sound of gun or rifle fire, but in half an hour or less the wood might be full of Germans. There were no trenches or shell-holes, we were beside a clear running stream, with tall poplars above our heads and spring flowers at our feet.

'It's a funny war,' I said. I thought he would know what I meant.

But he did not know. He looked at me, he saw my artillery badges, he was on foot, I was riding; he may have been the only survivor from his company. 'It may be for you,' he said, and the sound of his voice still hurts after more than fifty years, I hated his thinking that it had all been easy for us.

The battery was already across the river when I returned, Bingley had found a better place. He had just made the discovery that his revolver was lost, and he was nearly frantic. Now he would not be able to shoot himself if the enemy broke through. It was his servant's fault, he said; he always put the revolver at his side, within easy reach, when he went to sleep; but this morning his servant had moved it when he

48

brought in his cup of tea, and then in the hurry of getting off it had been left behind.

The loss of his revolver upset Bingley more than anything else that happened during the Retreat. He was not afraid of death, but he was afraid of being taken prisoner and he had made up his mind to shoot himself if the enemy broke through. Now there seemed a greater danger of this than before, we were in open country, it was just the place for a German cavalry attack.

He frightened us all with his nervousness, he kept on looking over his shoulder in the direction from which the Uhlans might be expected to appear. But it was all right. Sergeant Appleby, the captain of our football team and the most popular NCO in the battery, found a revolver and presented it to the grateful Bingley.

'You've saved my life,' he said to the smiling Appleby. This incident wiped out the memory of his lost chocolate on the previous day, and now Bingley had nothing but praise for our battery. 'You've only to look at Sergeant Appleby,' he said, 'to know that he's worth his weight in gold, and when you have good N.C.O.s you have a good battery.

He consulted Hughes, who as an ex-policemen, he thought, might know the best way of holding a revolver if you had to use it against yourself. But Hughes was no help to him. 'Can't say I've ever tried,' he said.

Revolvers were not the only things being found on this strange day. Army canteens and French estaminets were being abandoned, we all had full pockets, and bottles of wine fitted comfortably into the baskets meant for shells in the gun limbers. I myself had a bottle of red wine in each pocket of my British Warm overcoat. Cherry had given them to me, he had come out of the estaminet in which Brigade Headquarters had spent the night with his arms full of bottles. 'Pity to leave this good stuff for the Boche,' he said.

We were not the only people in retreat, all the villagers were on the move. I noticed one family with a dilapidated wagon piled high with furniture, an old woman was pushing a hand-cart and a little girl driving a black cow. Somehow the cow escaped, the girl ran after it, but was unable to recapture it, but it was easy for me on my horse to catch it and bring it back to her. She smiled at me. 'Merci, monsieur,' she said.

It was pleasurable at such a time to receive the smile of a nine-year-old child, but I was distressed by the plight of these refugees. I felt we had failed them. They were depending on us to keep the enemy away from their homes, but the enemy was coming. Retreating was a part of our job, but it was not theirs, they were losing nearly all that they had, the whole course of their lives was in danger. They were old people, old people and children, they were without the strong middle-aged group of their families, they seemed to have lost hope of better things. I saw an old man and his wife walking along a road under fire. A shell burst on their left, then one on the right, but they took no notice, they just walked on, looking neither to right nor left.

The Retreat went on.

But on this day we did not go back so far as on other days. In the evening we came to a village called Lavieville. Not one of the houses had yet been damaged by shellfire, but not one was inhabited, all the people had left. We chose a house for ourselves at the edge of the village, there was a long garden at the back and through a gate in the wall there was a way on to the road where our guns were.

The house had already been ransacked, the floors in every room were covered with old clothes and rubbish. Other soldiers had probably visited the house before we arrived. But it was a roof over our heads, it provided us with beds and with some of the other comforts of ordinary life, chairs, and a table to eat at. Bingley said he had forgotten what it was like to eat in a civilised manner.

Tired though we all were we did not immediately go to bed after dinner. There was the wine to drink. We sat up talking, the events of the last few days and nights were beginning to take shape in our minds, we saw them in order, no longer like the disconnected sequences of a dream. The wine gave us encouragement and new hope.

The next morning there was no order to retreat. During the afternoon Australian soldiers came up from behind, they went along the road past our guns, up towards the line. This was the first time I had seen Australians, they were unlike any of our own divisions, and on this first occasion I was not attracted by them. They were noisy and swaggering, they did not march along the road, they just walked, they seemed to be without any kind of discipline. But they looked very different from the exhausted infantry in front of us, the men we had seen coming back day after day. Towards evening they came back once more. At dusk I saw them coming over the skyline, they came through our guns as more than once they had done before. But this time the enemy was not following, they were coming back because they had been relieved, the line was holding, the Australians were there.

I stayed by the guns. I could hardly believe it was over. Only a week had passed since the battle started, but it seemed a lifetime ago and that we should go on retreating for ever. I stayed by the guns until it was too dark to see, I was still expecting to see a line of retiring infantry coming back in front. But no one came, there were only the ordinary sounds of war in front, the Retreat was over.

Now I could go. I walked through the narrow garden and into the house where the others already were. How ordinary everything had become again! Frank was writing to his girl, Bingley sitting quietly in a chair, he was not pacing up and down the room, he had not lost anything, and Griffith was waiting impatiently for the servants to bring in dinner. Only Hughes looked up when I came out of the darkness into the candle-lit room. 'We were just coming to look for you,' he said. 'Thought you might have forgotten the time.'

Six

April

The Retreat was over, but the memory of defeat remained and we waited anxiously for the beginning of the second round, knowing that one victory would not be enough for the enemy, he had to destroy us if he was to win the war.

All through the months that followed we were waiting. Every night, as I got into my sleeping bag, I was aware that I might be wakened in the morning by a fierce bombardment, the preliminary to the next German attack, and that would mean it was about to start again: another retreat, more danger and anxiety, utter weariness again. The Australians were fresh, their morale was high, but the finest soldiers in the world could not stand up to an attack in such overwhelming strength as that which had fallen on us on March 21st.

Bingley was wounded on the second morning after our arrival in Lavieville. Like many other things during his brief time with us it need not have happened. He was standing on the road by the guns, talking to Major Villiers of A, whose battery was now back in action at our side. The enemy was shelling the road, Villiers got down into one of the slit trenches we had dug the day before, and he advised Bingley to join him. But Bingley was not afraid of shells, and he remained standing there, talking and smoking his pipe. A shell burst a few yards from him, and he was seriously wounded.

He was carried into the house and our Scottish doctor at once came up from Brigade Headquarters. He was in a good deal of pain, but the doctor said he would be all right, so there was no need for us to feel distressed on his account. Even now he was fussing about a triviality. This time it was his pipe, he had dropped it when he was hit, they had carried him away without it. It must be on the road still, and it was a very special pipe, a birthday present from some aristocratic friend.

Hughes told him not to worry, if it was there we would find it and send it after him to the Casualty Clearing Station. But he had no intention of going to look for it. 'What a hope the man's got!' he said after he had been taken away. 'Jerry's been shelling the place all morning; does he really think anyone's going to look for his blasted pipe? Lady What's-a-name can buy him another.'

Bingley had been with us for 17 days. It seemed like 17 months. And in that time the morale of the battery had sunk to a lower level than ever before, far lower than after months of fighting and heavy casualties at Ypres. Yet he was a likeable man. It was his misfortune, and ours, that he was in command of a battery at a time of crisis.

Griffith also was wounded, a few days later. I was up at the O.P. when it happened, but the others told me that he was in too much of a hurry for his breakfast. They were all by the guns, the enemy was shelling the edge of the village, the others decided to wait until he stopped, but Griffith went on and was hit before he got to the house. We were fortunate in our casualties at this time. The rest of us were all of one kind, but Bingley and Griffith were different and would always have stuck out.

Jamieson came up from the wagon lines to take command, and at once we all relaxed. He gave orders when they were necessary, we could see they were necessary, there was no fuss, no fault-finding, and decisions once made were adhered to. Jamieson was reserved, even rather unfriendly, seldom joining in conversation with the rest of us, but we had confidence in him. We knew that he knew what to do.

But within a few days there were greater changes, affecting the whole brigade. Captain Jamieson was promoted to the rank of major, he left us and went to command B Battery in place of Major Cecil who was demoted and brought down to the rank of captain. This was because he had blown up his guns at the beginning of the Retreat, without justification it was considered, and not very effectively. Everyone knew it was Major John's doing, he was the real commander of our brigade, not the well-meaning Colonel Richardson. Major John disliked and despised Cecil. He told the Colonel that he would not serve in a brigade in which *that man* held the same rank as himself, and the Colonel gave in to him.

Major Villiers of A Battery had lost his guns at the same time, he had been the first to give the order for destruction, Cecil had merely followed his example, and John would have liked to treat Villiers in the same way. But his rank was substantive, he could not be brought down without a court martial; besides, he was the brother of an earl, and even Major John could not succeed in forcing the Colonel to abandon an earl's brother.

Captain Cecil came back to us, as our second-in-command, a position he had held once before. None of us especially liked him, but we were sorry for him and felt he had been unfairly treated. We got a new battery commander at the same time. Major Poland, who had been John's second-in-command, was himself a Yorkshireman and ought to have got on well in our battery, but he was tolerated rather than liked. He was friendly to everyone in fair weather, but apt to become morose at other times, and there was a streak of meanness in him. He drank a lot of whisky when someone else was paying for it. 'I'm a proper Yorkshireman,' he was fond of saying. "Take owt, pay for nowt! that's my motto.' The difference between himself and the other Yorkshiremen in the battery was that they only pretended to be mean.

But after Bingley we were not particular about our battery commander.

A few days later I was sent up to the O.P. on a 24-hour duty. I felt ill at ease when I was told to go, I had a presentiment of evil. There was nothing to account for my feeling, the O.P. was not in a particularly dangerous place, I had been there before, and except on the day when Bingley was wounded, we had not been shelled much, it had been quiet since the end of our retreat.

But though there was no reason for my foreboding the feeling was very strong, and after leaving the battery in the late afternoon I turned round for a last look before we went over the crest, wondering if I should ever see the place again. This was a sop to superstition in which I often indulged, hoping that it might somehow increase my chance of a safe return.

Our walk up to the O.P. was so uneventful, however, that I

began to forget my fears, and the officer in B Battery whom I relieved told me that it had been as peaceful for the whole of his time. Visibility was poor, it had been misty all day, and now at six o'clock from the O.P. trench at the top of the hill I could hardly see down to the railway embankment, half a mile away, which was our front line. Beyond the railway was the river, the Ancre; beyond the river, the wooded marsh. It was the place where Bingley had sent me to reconnoitre the river crossing, the place where I had spoken to the infantry captain.

On a clear day you could see all the high ground on the other side, on the left you could almost see the little town of Albert, up the river and now in German hands. Almost but not quite, the town itself was hidden by a curve of the bare hill on which the O.P. was situated, but on my first visit I had seen the roof of the church over the hill and the diving madonna. She was one of the sights of the war zone. She had been hit by German shells before the battle of the Somme started, so that with the infant Jesus in her arms she looked about to plunge into the street below. There was a superstition that we should lose the war if she fell and the Engineers had propped her up in this diving position. But now she had fallen, our own big guns had brought her down after the enemy's capture of Albert.

Twenty-four hours was a long time, and we made a bad start. My signallers had brought up a dud telephone. They were a very inexperienced pair, a boy who had joined us shortly before the Retreat, and an elderly man who had come only since it ended. They should not have been sent out together, but because of casualties we were short of signallers. I should have to send one of them back to the battery for another telephone. But the boy said he could not find the way in the dark and the man said he was afraid of going by himself. He was in a pitiable state, literally shaking with fear; it was his first visit to an O.P. and he had never been under fire. I felt exasperated with him, we were in no danger at all, we might have been sitting on the grass in England. 'Stop being such a bloody funk,' I wanted to say to him, but I remembered in time that it was less than a year since I had been new to the War, and I had been afraid before there was anything to fear. I sent them both back, and they were better when they returned, the older man had stopped shaking, they had achieved something, they had achieved it on their own, and this had given them confidence.

The night passed very slowly. The mist turned to drizzling rain, my signallers were dozing in the shallow trench, but I walked up and down all night, counting the hours by the number of cigarettes I smoked and allowing myself a mouthful of rum every hour. It kept me warm, I was getting very wet.

Daylight made a reluctant appearance, but I continued to walk up and down. The rain had stopped, but it was too misty for me to see, or to be seen from the enemy O.P.s on the other hillside. Shortly before seven o'clock, however, the mist thinned out and I got down into the trench. Now I could see down to the railway embankment and the trees in the valley, and dimly the shape of the high ground across the river.

I was standing there, looking down at the valley, but not consciously seeing anything, not consciously thinking at all, when suddenly every nerve in my body was alerted by the opening roar of bombardment across the river. My presentiment had been right, the attack was coming. A moment ago there had been utter silence, all the valley at peace, now every gun on the other side was firing and I saw bursting shells wherever I looked.

For the moment we were in no danger. The shells were falling in front of us, astride the railway embankment, our front line, or passing overhead on their way to the batteries and our reserves. None fell near us, our telephone line was not broken yet, I was able to speak to Cherry at Brigade Headquarters, to watch what was happening, to look out for any movement in the valley. For half an hour I was watching, watching and waiting. Then I heard a different sound, the sound of a shell coming close, and I crouched down in the trench.

I have called it a trench, but in fact it was nothing more than a hole in the ground. A trench with its depth and narrow opening would have afforded us protection from anything but a direct hit; but this hole was less than two feet deep and wide at the top. Any shell falling within fifty yards might have killed us all and during the next hour and a half at least a dozen burst very close. Now that danger had come my signallers behaved admirably. The young one brought out his rations and began to eat, the older one sat quite still beside me. He probably thought it was like this every morning at the O.P. No wonder he had been scared. He was frightened of course, but no more so than myself. Indeed in his relief at finding that he could endure, that he did not have to scream or feel he was going mad he may have been less afraid than I was. At any rate he was all right and he continued to be all right for the rest of his time in the battery.

I was very afraid, knowing how great our danger was. I was expecting death, and the expectation paralysed my mind. My eyes were open, my hearing was very acute, I heard each shell coming towards us and could tell where it was likely to burst from the sound it made.

My senses were alert, but I could not think or speak, I did not reply to the signaller at my side. I just waited for death, pressing myself more closely to the earth whenever I heard a near shell on its way. Then I felt the ground shake, heard the iron splinters whizz past us, smelled the fumes of the explosion, saw the dark smoke drifting overhead.

I watched a family of frogs as I waited. They had appeared from somewhere, the noise was frightening them and they were trying to get out of the hole. Again and again they jumped, they very nearly succeeded, but always fell back again when nearly at the top. I could have told them they were safer where they were, and I wondered whether to put them back if they did succeed.

Then the sound changed again. I became aware that shells were no longer falling round us. This was the critical time: now the enemy was attacking and therefore his guns could not shell the area over which his infantry was expected to advance. I stood up and looked down into the valley. At first I saw no one, there was no movement on the railway embankment nor in the wooded valley. But before there was time to think out what this might mean I saw men getting up on the railway line. They were Australians, not Germans. They did not appear to be in trouble, they were not being fired at, none of them fell, but I saw them come down from the embankment and start to climb the hill towards me. Still I could see

57

no enemy. But the Australians were coming up the hill. This was what we had seen day after day during the Retreat, our men coming back, then the enemy following, and I had no doubt that it was about to happen again. I sent my signallers back with written messages, first one, then the other, the telephone line had been broken long since, but I waited where I was for the Australians.

They were a long time coming. They came up the hill very slowly. They were not firing, or being fired at, I could see no Germans, but the view on my left was blocked by the curve of the hill, I could only see directly in front. At last the men drew level with me and I asked the nearest of them what was happening.

'The bastards on our left let the bastards in,' he said.

'We got a lot of the bastards,' another man added.

An officer told me that the battalion on their left had been driven back, and that they themselves in consequence had been ordered to fall back to the crest of the hill behind me. It was time for me to go, I went back to Brigade Headquarters, which was nearer to the line than the batteries were, I gave Cherry a gloomy report on the situation. None of the Australians had seemed despondent, but they did not know what it was going to be like, they had not experienced a retreat, I thought my pessimism was justified.

But once again Cherry was better informed than I was, this time not because of Major John, but because he was in touch with the Headquarters of the Australian Infantry Battalion, which was in the same hillside. He said the situation was well in hand, that our battalion had repulsed the attack on its front, and though it had fallen back now it was about to take part in a counter-attack.

I did not believe him, I thought that as usual he was making the news seem better than it was. But the Australians did counter-attack, they regained nearly all the lost ground, our battalion returned to the railway line. Cherry wanted me to go back to the O.P., but I could not yet return to that hole of fear, my mind had not recovered. I went instead to another hilltop looking down on the railway embankment and wooded marsh, but without such an extensive view across the valley. Major John sent one of his officers to the original O.P. during the afternoon, but his signaller was killed there, so I thought my unwillingness to return had been justified.

Nothing else happened that day.

The German attack had failed. It was not a major attack, as I had at first supposed, only a minor one, but it had failed. The enemy had gained nothing, we were still in the same position, the Australians had shown that their confidence in themselves was justified, and we began to share it.

A few days later we were taken out of the line, into a reserve position. We were relieved by an Australian battery, and Major Poland sent me up to the O.P. with their commander to show him where it was. We walked up there together, and because I liked him and wanted to make a good impression I was pleased at being able to answer all his questions. I could tell him the names of all the places behind the enemy line and show him where they were on the map. I also told him about our very unpleasant time there, the hole had been made a little deeper now, but he agreed with me that more work should be done on it.

The rest of the battery had already gone when we returned. I was to complete the relief, there were certain things that had to be explained to the Australians, a few stores to hand over. They were critical of what we had done, but every battery on taking over a position always criticised the work of their predecessors, it was part of the routine. When this was finished I went into the mess to wait for Edric, who was coming up with our horses. It was their mess now, ours no longer. We had moved out of Lavieville, the village had become too dangerous. We had brought the guns a few hundred yards back, they were under a bank in which we had dug shelters for ourselves. The mess was the largest and most comfortable of these.

Three or four of the Australian officers were in the mess and I listened to their conversation. They were talking about the German attack in the North, in Flanders. On the same day that he had attacked us in the river valley the enemy had made a major attack up there and already it had met with great success. The Australians had just come from Flanders, from the very place where the new attack was being made.

'Fritz waited till he knew we were out of the way,' one of them said.

'These Britishers are no good,' said another.

'Shut up!' said the Captain who had been at the O.P. with me.

'Well, look where they've run to! We should never have run like that.'

'You don't know what you're talking about,' said the Captain. 'We've never had to face an attack like one of these.'

But the other insisted that the English had no fighting spirit.

I was so angry at what they were saying that I got up, intending to walk out of the dug-out, but I was faint from lack of food, I had eaten nothing all day except a slice of bread and marmalade, I staggered and had to sit down again. At once their attitude changed, and my own opinion of Australians changed for ever in the same moment. The Captain told his servant to make tea straight away, and the man who had said that Britishers ran away got up and opened a bottle of red wine, and we all drank together.

'That's only our way of talking,' he said. 'We talk big, but you mustn't pay any attention to what we say.'

I learnt not to. It's what people are that matters, what they do, not what they say. During the weeks that followed I often heard the Australians talking big, but I no longer minded. They were magnificent soldiers, and when I was in need they never failed to help me.

I enjoyed my tea and was feeling a new man by the time Edric came for me. I did not join the rest of the battery that night, I was to stay with a single gun a short way in front of the others. Vernon of B Battery had one of his guns in the same place. We spent the night together in a wayside shrine by the road. Vernon was a friend of mine; I was always pleased when chance brought us together. I had friends in all the other batteries, but there had been no opportunity of talking to any of them since the beginning of the Retreat. Now I could talk to Vernon, he told me all his battery news and I told him ours as we lay side by side on the narrow tiled floor of the shrine. Our conversation was entirely about the war, about the events of the last two or three weeks and the other officers in the brigade. If there had been less to say on that subject we might have talked on another, but we could have talked all night without wearying each other, it was talking about the War that helped us to endure it.

'We mustn't forget to thank Mary,' Vernon said in the morning. 'She couldn't have protected us from shells, but she's done what she could, she's kept us warm during the night.' We had both slept well. It was a strange place in which to wake: the painted stars on the domed ceiling of the shrine over our heads, the blue-mantled madonna looking down on us from her niche in the wall, outside the distant muttering of the guns and the deserted country road between two villages.

Later in the day we rejoined our batteries. They were almost out of range of gunfire, but we were in readiness to return at an hour's notice if there was another attack. Our tents were by the side of a wood, there were bluebells in it and enormous cowslips in the meadows. I had never seen France looking so beautiful. I had never looked at Spring until now, I had always taken it for granted. This year it might have come too late for me to see it, and I might not see another. I looked at the young leaves on the trees, I had not known that anything could be so lovely.

It was while we were resting by the bluebell wood that the men who had been on leave during the Retreat came back to us, Jack and Durham, Sergeant Denmark and more than twenty others. They made us up to strength again. They came marching into camp one afternoon, looking rather sheepish, like boys who had been playing truant and did not know what kind of reception they would be given. We cheered when we saw them and their faces broke into smiles.

'We thought we should be sent to another unit,' Jack said, when we were having tea in the mess, 'we thought you would all be dead, or prisoners anyway.'

We told them everything that had happened, we were all talking at the same time, and at the end Jack told us what he had been doing. 'It was a rotten leave,' he said. 'I was thinking about you all the time. I went out with a girl once or twice, but it was no good, I couldn't do a thing. You can't even get any kick out of kissing a girl when you're thinking that all your friends have gone west.'

He said he had felt miserable all the time, and not only because girls had been unsatisfying. 'You can't talk to people at home,' he said. 'They haven't a clue what it means, even the best of them, and some of them think of it as a kind of entertainment.' Someone, he told us, had suggested going up to Beachy Head for a picnic, so as to hear the guns. 'I said I'd heard them,' Jack said. And someone else had asked whether he had ever taken part in a battle. 'They don't call this sort of thing a battle,' he said. 'They think you have to be drawn up in squares, facing each other.'

'I'm sorry I missed it,' Durham said, as we were undressing that night. 'It must have been rather fun.'

'It wasn't,' I told him. 'It wasn't funny at all.' But now that it was over I was glad myself not to have missed it.

We were still in the same place when the Commander-in-Chief issued his famous Backs-to-the-Wall Order of the Day, which, it has sometimes been claimed, had such a stirring effect on us. We read it. 'Many of us are now tired,' Frank quoted. 'Has he only just found that out?' I never saw any of our men reading it, but they may have done so, for Sergeant Denmark said we seemed to have got ourselves into a proper mess while he was away. 'It's about time we chucked up the sponge,' he told me.

He was always grumbling, nothing was any bloody good in his opinion. But I knew he would be the last to give in, he would go on fighting and enduring to the end, and I always felt a braver man when I was with him.

We did not go back to Lavieville when our short rest came to an end. We were attached to a different Australian division, we were sent a few miles south of where we had been before. Now we were between the rivers, the Somme in front of us, the Ancre at our back.

Another great attack was expected, it might come any day now. We were digging hard. The guns were out in the open, near the top of the hill above the Ancre. We were living in two copses growing out of little round hollows, into the sides of which we could dig. Hughes and I were making a shelter, four feet wide, long enough to lie down in, as deep as we could dig it. Hughes was as good with a spade as he was with most other things. 'Tisn't exactly comfortable,' he said, 'some people might prefer Buckingham Palace, but we want less roof space.'

Any day now the attack was expected, the great German offensive which was to complete what they had begun, to drive us into the sea, to cut between ourselves and the French Armies. So when very early one morning we were awakened by a great enemy bombardment I never doubted that the day had come. Shells were falling all round us, gas and high explosive. We lay very still in our hole, we had put our boots on and were ready to rush out to the guns when the SOS rockets went up, the signal that the enemy was attacking and for us to open fire.

But the rockets did not go up, and gradually the bombardment died down. On our front only a small attack had been made, and had been easily repulsed. Across the river Somme, however, on our right, the attack had been much heavier, we learnt, and Villers Bretonneux at the highest point of the plateau above the river had been lost. This was a disaster. From the village you could look down on the spire of Amiens Cathedral, only nine miles away. We should have to retreat again, Amiens could never be held with the enemy in Villers Bretonneux, and many of our positions between the rivers were now under observation.

But that night it was recaptured. The Australians made a night attack, one force going round the village on the north side and another on the south. They met in the middle, then turned back and overran the enemy positions inside, killing or capturing every German there. They had done it again, the Australians had done it again, for the second time they had completely defeated a German attack.

We were all jubilant. Cherry and Colonel Richardson talked as though the War was as good as won, disregarding the huge advance which the enemy had made in Flanders and the fact that the major attack on our front had not yet been made.

'We've only got to kill another million Boches,' the Colonel said. 'Then we shall all be able to go home.'

I thought I had killed one on my last visit to the OP, and

Durham caught some ammunition wagons that had come up too near the line before it was dark. He said he got in among them with three or four salvoes.

We were jubilant about Villers Bretonneux, but there was no other reason for rejoicing. Another great attack was certain to be made, and even the Australians would be driven back by the hordes of the enemy. There was nothing to look forward to, all leave had been cancelled, there was no chance of our going out of the line for a rest, there was not even a town within reach where we could go for a dinner or to laugh at one of the divisional entertainments; and winter, which might put an end to the fighting for a while, was still months away.

'I suppose it will be another Hundred Years War,' Jack said.

Seven

May-June

April was passing into May. Riding down to the wagon lines one afternoon I saw swallows circling above the river, and the beech leaves fully out over my head were rustling in the light wind as I dried myself after my bath. I had got rid of the lice on my body, but what about those on my clothes?

All through May we were waiting for the Germans to come. The Australians were not passively waiting, they ruled over no-man's-land by night, they harassed the enemy by raiding his trenches. Fritz was going to get the surprise of his life when he came, they said.

We had to leave our copses in the little rounded hollows above the river, they attracted too much attention from the enemy. We had just begun dinner one evening, we had finished the soup and were waiting for the servants to bring in the main course when a heavy bombardment began. I hoped it would be nothing serious, a few salvoes, a dozen shells altogether. Then we could go on with our dinner, I was hungry. But as soon as it became clear that the shelling was not going to stop, I moved to the back of the dug-out, with my back to the wall of chalk, and went on writing the letter I had started before dinner.

The men were in one of the copses, the officers and our servants and the signallers in the other. The men had one good dug-out in their copse, we had one in ours, all the servants and signallers were inside it now with ourselves, about a dozen of us, all crowded together, no one talking, or in such subdued voices that only the man next to the speaker could hear what he said. Most of us would have been killed or seriously wounded if one of the shells had hit the roof, but we were probably safe from anything except a direct hit.

65

It was disagreeable. Shells were coming over at the rate of two or three to the minute, we were shaken by the concussion, we could hear trees and branches falling, but I was not particularly frightened. It was when one was alone that shellfire was so frightening, or when one was under fire in the open. Now we were all together, there was nothing that had to be done until the shellfire was over, and the back of the dug-out was the safest place. I went on writing.

But Durham was standing in the entrance, rather foolishly because there he was more likely to be hit by a flying splinter. He was watching the shell-bursts and telling us where each one was. 'That was a better one,' he would say, meaning a nearer one; and then as though giving orders to the German gunners, 'Five minutes more right.' I could see that Major Poland sitting at the table was growing restless. He had been inside a dug-out when it was hit some months before, and his wounds had recovered more quickly than his nerves.

A shell burst very close. The earth shook, bits of chalk off the wall fell on my writing pad, the wood was full of smoke and the smell of cordite. There was silence. Then we all heard Durham's drawling voice stating the obvious. 'That one was not very far away,' he said.

'If you have nothing more sensible to say, keep your bloody mouth shut,' said Poland angrily.

Durham and I grinned at each other when he wasn't looking.

It stopped at last. I was suddenly conscious of the silence, there was no shell on its way through the air. I looked at my watch, it had lasted eighty minutes. We all began talking at the same time, waiting where we were for another minute in case he was playing us a dirty trick. Then we ran across to the other copse to see how the men were. One man had been wounded, not very seriously.

But our dinner had gone. So had the cook-house.

As soon as it was light the next morning Major Poland took me with him to look for another battery position. He had had enough of those copses to last him a million years, he said, and he blamed himself for choosing a place marked on all their maps, of course they could not resist shooting at it. He decided to leave two guns where they were, the men

66

must dig deep slit trenches beside them, but he found a place for the other four behind a bank half way down the hill. It was annoying when we had put so much effort into our digging in the copses, now we should have to begin all over again; but Poland's decision was a wise one, and we were not so heavily shelled under the bank.

After a quick breakfast I went up to the O.P. and spent the rest of the day there. In retrospect I seem to have spent most of the long summer at that O.P. on the high ground between the rivers, looking down on the Somme. It was the loneliness of the OP that made the days there seem so long, the loneliness and the width of the view. It was in a short piece of trench high above the village of Sailly-le-Sec, and you could see all the world—the Somme, a long straight silver line in the middle of the picture, villages and church spires among the trees in the valley; and then mile after mile of rising upland, more villages, and trees on the skyline, marking the long straight Roman Road, the road from Villers Bretonneux to Peronne and St Quentin, places utterly remote, so far were they now behind the German line.

At first the country looked undamaged. Until a few weeks ago it had been far behind our line and never fought over. Now we were beginning to destroy it, we and the enemy between us, shelling the villages, cratering the fields, killing the trees; but the concentration of guns was not nearly so great as at Ypres in 1917, and even by the end of the summer, even in the front line area, villages from a distance still looked almost untouched and there were far more living trees than dead ones.

At first there was a lot of activity behind the German lines —men digging or walking about, lorries and wagons on the roads, horses in their wagon line area, even the smoke of a distant train. Few of these targets were within range of our field guns, occasionally I saw a party of men to shoot at, more often I had to ring up Cherry at Brigade Headquarters and ask him to ask for the use of some longer-range guns. Nothing ever happened, none of my distant targets was disturbed. The fact was there were very few heavy guns in action on our part of the front, some had been lost in the March Retreat, and the fear of losing others in the next attack kept them well back, field guns were expendable, bigger guns were not. This was another reason why the country looked unspoiled, our small guns could be very effective against infantry in the open, but they did little damage to anything else.

Eventually I stopped reporting what I saw, and after the first few weeks there was less to report. All that vast expanse of country in front of me, and no living creature to be seen on it!

But there were aeroplane fights to watch, particularly in the late afternoon. That was the time for the dog fights. I was watching half a dozen of our machines one evening returning from a sortie over enemy territory. They were crossing the line when suddenly I heard fierce bursts of machine-gun fire and German triplanes swooped down on them out of the clouds. I had not seen the triplanes until the firing began, neither had they. It was all over in a moment, two of our machines were on fire, a third was fluttering down to the ground, like a leaf in autumn, the enemy was away again.

Three out of six! I felt sick with anger and frustration, I would rather have endured a period of heavy shell-fire in my trench than be the witness of such a tragedy. Two spirals of black smoke against the evening sky, and the other machine still falling, so slowly, that it seemed it would never reach the ground. It fell beside the river, in no-man's-land, less than a mile from where I was watching. There it lay. It looked undamaged. Surely it would rise again, like a bird after alighting. But it lay still, between the armies. No one got out, no one went towards it, only the river moved, flowing serenely by.

But an hour or two later I saw a huge explosion far behind the enemy line, ten miles away. A great column of smoke rose hundreds of feet into the air, and I counted twenty smaller explosions. That was some consolation for the lost aeroplanes, but on every subsequent visit to the O.P. I was reminded of the unhappiness of that evening by the sight of the aeroplane, still lying where it had fallen, the fluttering leaf that had reached the ground.

All through those long summer days in that long summer I stood in the little trench above the river, gazing and gazing through my glasses at the enemy-held country until my eyes ached and I could look no more. I learnt the names of every wood and all the villages, I knew the contour of the hills and the shape of the lakes in the valley. To see so much and to see nothing! We might have been the only men left alive, my two signallers and I. And yet I knew there were thousands of hidden men in front of me. Australians on our side of the line, the enemy on his. But no one moved, everyone was waiting for the safety of darkness.

Once or twice I left the safety of the trench and went out alone, down the hill towards Sailly-le-Sec. The ground fell away steeply below the O.P., but then rose again, so that one was swallowed up within a few minutes of leaving the trench. I told myself that I might obtain some useful information, there might be a company or battalion headquarters in one of the gullies, but in fact I wanted companionship, to hear another voice. But I saw no one, and it was frightening. I was afraid of losing my way, of not being able to find the O.P. again, I might take a wrong turning and wander into the German lines. There was a story of an Australian barber who had ridden up on a bicycle from the transport lines, he wanted to see the place where his friends were, but he went too far, he rode into the enemy.

I stopped going out on these adventures. I talked to my own signallers instead, I read my book. I reckoned I could read a book in a day at the O.P., the kind of book I took with me, I did not feel able to read any other sort.

At last it was time to return to the battery. One was supposed to stay up at the O.P. until it was too dark to see, but I came away at dusk, or even a little sooner if the enemy was not shelling the top of the ridge behind us. Choosing a quiet moment one got out of the trench and walked quickly up the hill. The first half mile in the evening, the last half mile in the morning, that was the dangerous part, one was under observation, and a party of three men might be worth shooting at. Once or twice I thought we were chased with shells. But over the skyline one relaxed. Now there was the evening meal to look forward to, hearing what sort of a day the others had had, and telling them about my own.

A long day at the O.P. but then, if one was lucky, two or three days and nights at the wagon lines.

Edric would come for me with our horses in the late afternoon, and then there was the enjoyment of the long ride back, cantering at first until we were out of the danger zone, more slowly when we were across the river and marsh. Edric would ride beside me as we walked up the hill on the other side, telling me the news of the wagon lines—the night bombers had been over, the Australians had been pinching horses from some of the other batteries, we should have to watch out for Lady with so many horse thieves about, and there was a craze for playing Housey-Housey, some of the men played every fine afternoon; he explained the game to me.

The wagon lines were a long way back. Across the Ancre, up the hill, over the Albert-Amiens road, and then the wood was in sight, the tops of the trees showing above the skyline. The horse lines and the men's bivouacs were under a bank below the wood, our tents at the wood's edge. It was a delightful change to be there: to undress and sleep on a camp bed, to be wakened in the morning not by shellfire but by the trumpeter blowing reveille, to bath, and then to spend most of the day doing what one liked.

There was some work for us to do at the wagon lines, but not a great deal. I went out riding, chiefly for pleasure, also to learn my way about the country, such knowledge might be useful one day; and as mess secretary it was my job to buy whatever luxuries I could find, eggs, a chicken, lettuce. The French farmers would sell us anything they had, and there were army canteens in the back areas.

I also drew money from the Field Cashier, for ourselves and to pay the men. Paying was not difficult for me. The others sometimes got into a muddle when they were paying, they might be a hundred francs out at the end of the afternoon; but Bombardier Ewell, the battery clerk, and I were both confident that the amounts would balance when I was paying. I was quick at mental arithmetic, there were plenty of things the others could do better than myself, I knew little about horses, I was no good at roofing a dug-out or repairing a gun, but I could add up correctly.

I enjoyed paying because it brought me into contact with all the men at the wagon lines, there were always some gunners among them as well as the drivers, they took it in

70

turns to come down, as we ourselves did. I found it difficult to talk to some of the men, difficult even to understand what they said. My upbringing had been different from theirs, I shared the War with them, but little else at that time. But I wanted to make them aware of my friendship for them, and smiling as I paid them was a way of showing my feeling.

In the evening I talked to Captain Cecil. I had been expecting to feel some embarrassment in his company; he had been a major, now he was only a captain, we had called him Sir, but one did not sir a captain; I thought it would be difficult to be natural with him. But he showed an unexpected dignity, accepting the situation and making no attempt to assert authority over us when we came down to the wagon lines for a rest. I had liked him before, and I liked him again now.

He was bitter about Major John, who was responsible for his degradation. He said that John had given the Colonel an untrue account of what happened that night at Heudecourt, and that the Colonel had allowed him no chance of replying to his accusations. I could well believe that Major John's personal dislike of Cecil had influenced what he said, but not that he had invented a story in order to discredit him. Cecil believed the worst of Major John, but I knew that I admired him more than anyone else in the brigade.

We sat up late into the night, talking not only about the War and other officers in the brigade, but about life in England, the life that some day we might go back to. Cecil was nearly ten years older than I was, already a partner in his father's firm, and married on his last leave—he told me he was hoping to become a father before the end of the year. But he treated me as an equal and I was pleased. Talking to him at the wagon lines, sometimes for an hour or two I almost forgot the great German attack we were waiting for.

The wood closed round us as we talked, and the stars came nearer.

May was passing into June. The young corn behind the guns was several inches high, and the sun rose so early that however early I got up I never arrived at the O.P. before daylight, there was always that last half mile to walk down the hill under observation.

The enemy made his great attack, the third he had made since March. But it was not on our part of the front, it was made on the French front between Rheims and Soissons, against the French and four unfortunate British divisions, which had been sent to a supposedly quiet part of the line after suffering very severe casualties in the earlier attacks.

I was sorry for the French, they were being driven back as we had been, Paris was in danger for a while, but I was thankful that we had escaped for the present. It was only a respite. Everyone believed that the attack on the French was only a diversion, to draw our reserves away from the vital front, the enemy knew that he must defeat the British before he could win the war. But for a few weeks at any rate we should be left alone, he could not mount another attack without a pause.

Major John was killed. The camouflage over one of his guns was set alight by the heat of its own firing, and there was a lot of ammunition by the side of the gun. He ordered everyone else to leave the position, but he stayed, fighting the fire single-handed until the ammunition blew up.

He ought to have known this would happen, his own subalterns could have told him. And what would the loss of a gun have mattered, or all the ammunition in the brigade! Guns and ammunition could be replaced, Major John never was.

But D Battery, his battery, was a howitzer battery, most of his service had been in 18-pounder batteries, he had only been with D for a few months, since recovering from his last wound, he did not realise that howitzer ammunition was more likely to blow up, he had not deliberately thrown away his life.

Nearly everyone, now that he was dead, began to speak well of him and to tell stories of his courage. Even the Australians admired him. They said they did not want to go about in his company, he was too much of a glory-boy for their liking. They all knew him by sight, everyone knew him because he went everywhere, he was always going up to the front line, to see for himself, to find out what he wanted to

72

know. His officers said that he was often out all night, he liked to see the sun rise over the enemy lines, they said, he had told them that it filled him with exhilaration.

They said he was mad, everyone agreed that he was mad, but everyone was proud of having known him, we boasted about him, he became a legendary figure. Only Captain Cecil remained of the same opinion as before. Others could say what they liked, he said, but he wasn't going to pretend that he had admired Major John or was sorry he was dead.

I had met him on my way up to the O.P. one morning, not long before his death. He had not spoken to me, but he had acknowledged my salute with a tight smile in which there was no unfriendly look. He was not a glory-boy, he did not love danger or glory, he despised both. But he had set himself a standard and he had to live up to it. He could not accept anything that fell below it, never for himself, hardly for anyone else. He was the greatest soldier I was ever to serve with.

Colonel Richardson was now free to do as he liked. He had told Cecil that he could feel no confidence in him as a battery commander, but he put him in command of our battery now, Poland went back to command D, the battery from which he had come, and Frank became a captain and our second-in-command.

The rest of us were not altogether pleased with these changes. We had liked Captain Cecil well enough, but we wondered how we should get on with Major Cecil. He cared too much about his own comfort, he was a selfish man, and there was no room for selfishness in a small dug-out. After himself he seemed to care more for his dog than for anyone else. She was a black-and-white setter, far too big an animal for the gun line, she was always in the way. Everyone in the battery was waiting for the day when she would get in the way of a shell, but Betty, like her master, knew how to look after herself.

The long summer passed slowly. Days in the gun line, followed by days at the wagon lines. Away from the smell of the dead mule and the smell of gas-drenched grass, away from the Seven Sisters, seven trees (only six now) by our two forward guns, away from shells and the ceaseless rumble of gun-fire—down to the silences of the wood and the clean

73

smell of midsummer. But even at the wagon lines we had bombing raids, twice a night sometimes when the moon was shining, one of my drivers was killed; and the weight of summer had taken the place of the lightness of spring.

We also lost a number of horses and in the last year of the war it was almost as difficult to get good remounts, as replacement horses were called, as to get good men. Sometimes we had to accept mules, which could survive in worse conditions than horses and on less food. But in C Battery we were fortunate or favoured and to the end of the war we remained nearly one hundred per cent horse-drawn. The drivers of course loved their horses, but every man in the battery was proud of their good looks. Our horses made us believe in ourselves, gave us confidence that we were a good battery.

There were two great beautiful cart horses, Billy and Prince, the one a chestnut, the other black, that went every afternoon with a G.S. Wagon (general service) to draw our rations for the next day from the nearest dump. Prince was killed in one of the night bombing raids on the wagon lines and we all felt poorer.

For a while I was on less friendly terms with Frank than I had been before. He was happier than I had ever known him, but he seemed to have gone over to the other side now that he was a captain, Cecil's side against ours. A captain's pay was considerably better than a lieutenant's, he could afford marriage now. But besides this, a captain's job was the safest in a battery of Field Artillery, he had a better chance now of surviving.

'I don't intend to take any more risks than I can help,' he said to me one evening. 'I consider that I've done my share of fighting, I've had nearly three years of it.'

How could any of us believe we had done our share until the War was over! I at any rate had done so little as yet.

'You'll have done your share too,' he said, 'by the end of this year.'

I thought I should probably be killed before the end of the year. I had not thought so at first, but now I was losing confidence in my chance of survival. One had a lot of lucky escapes, but there came a day when one's guardian angel was not looking, his back was turned, and in that moment it happened. My luck could not last for ever, I'd had my share of lucky escapes, even in the last few weeks there had been two —the sniper's bullet at Maricourt, the near misses in the shallow O.P., the hole of fear, on the hillside above the river.

Up to the guns again. Back to the Seven Sisters (only five now) and the untended green cornfields, back to the noise and dirt and discomfort, to the sickly smell of the gas-drenched grass in the valley, and the smell of the dead mule —it was a guide on a dark night between our main position and the two forward guns.

We were making a mine dug-out at the forward section, each of us spent a night up there in turn. I liked to work with the men when it was my turn. Every one of them knew more than myself about the construction of a mine dug-out, I was the most unskilled labourer. They took no notice of me, they talked as though I was not there, but I was one of them, I knew they trusted me.

How airless it was in the deep mine dug-out! The candles flickered and then went out. When this happened the man nearest to the top of the steps lifted the gas curtain and looked out, shouting down to the rest of us whether it was night or morning. If it was morning we came up, yawning, smelling the freshness of the day outside. Even the gas-soaked cornfields were fresher in the dawn than the air at the bottom of the dug-out. Then sleep.

June was passing into July. The dry fields were splashed with scarlet poppies.

June was the first month in which the enemy had made no major attack. Why was he waiting?

The Australians were preparing an attack of their own. They were going to show the enemy that they also had the power to dictate events. It was not to be a major attack. Not yet. The village of Hamel, between the Somme and Villers Bretonneux, was the objective. The village was on a ridge that looked down on the Australian positions, it hampered their movements, it would certainly make a general advance

75

more difficult if at some later time that was decided on. Hamel and the Vaire Wood ridge were to be captured. An American battalion was to take part in the attack. On the Fourth of July, American Independence Day. It would almost be the first time that American soldiers had been in action, it would be the first time ever that they had fought side by side with ourselves.

Our brigade was ordered to move forward into the valley of the Somme. We moved by night. The guns were to be silent until the morning of the attack, we were so close to the front line that we could not even walk about on the position by day, we were under observation from Vaire Wood. The guns were in front of a bank, they were covered with branches of trees to make them look like part of the brushwood. We used fresh branches every night, bad camouflage was worse than none at all, it showed you were trying to hide something.

We worked through the short summer nights, digging shelters, putting away and concealing the ammunition which had come up, covering our tracks with grass. After the night's work we slept. Though we were so close to the line it was one of the quietest places I ever was in. The little village of Vaux nearly hidden in trees was in front of us, on our right two hundred yards away the road leading to the village, and on the other side of the road the marsh began, river and lakes and marsh, together they formed the valley, and somewhere in the valley was our front line, somewhere his. Our position was hardly shelled at all. Sometimes in the afternoon it was so quiet that you expected to hear Vaux church bell ringing, or the clock striking the hour.

'Come for a bathe in the lake,' Durham said when I woke up one afternoon. I refused, it seemed madness to bathe so close to the enemy. But he would not let me alone.

'You said you were longing for a bathe.'

'You said how hot and sticky you felt.'

'You can't let B Battery think they're better than we are, they've been bathing.'

'Anything
B can do
C can do
Better,' he sang at me.

76

He made me go with him. We had to crawl through the long grass down to the road, but we were safe when we got there, the tall trees in the valley hid us from the enemy's view. We walked down to the lake, we looked for and found a place where the water was deep at the edge and there were no reeds; we undressed, we dived into the clear cool water.

'Don't splash so much,' I said. 'They'll hear us.'

He turned over on to his back and kicked his legs in the air. We dived again and again, we swam out towards the middle of the lake, the water was all a-glitter in the bright sunshine. Afterwards we sat on the bank, dangling our legs in the water, feeling the warmth on our naked bodies, hearing the water's lap against the reeds and the gentle breeze at the top of the poplars and silver willows.

We went there each afternoon. I almost forgot that I was a soldier, I became a boy again. We were out of uniform, for the moment we had no responsibilities, we need not even think about the war until nightfall. The fact that we were close to the enemy even added to our enjoyment, we were like boys from school who have deliberately broken bounds and are half hoping to hear a master's voice for the excitement of having to escape from him.

We had our excitement one afternoon, for while we were dressing a German gun opened fire on the valley. We were in no real danger, we were not in the line of the shells, we were completely hidden from sight by the tall trees on the other side of the lake. A lot of the shells fell into water, bursting on percussion and sending great spouts of water twenty or thirty feet into the air. We laughed, it was a spectacular display.

'Very poor shooting!' Durham said. 'No points at all!'

The war was like a game to him, a game not to be enjoyed, but to be won. He was always giving points to our side: for bathing in the face of the enemy, 3 points; for watching his shells burst in the water and do no harm to anyone, 3 more. He never allowed the enemy any points at all. Nothing could destroy his gaiety, he was the only one of us who never became depressed. His slow deliberate voice, his laughter, his healthy good-looking face—he was worth a lot of points to our battery.

We were malicious enough to enjoy our bathes even more because of Major Cecil's discomfiture. He wanted to come with us, but had not the courage to do so. Instead, he walked back more than a mile and bathed in the River Ancre, and the long double walk in the heat of the day, or as he said, the presence of mustard gas in the water gave him a bad headache and he could not eat his dinner. We still had the natural cruelty of boys.

Zero Hour was at ten minutes past three on the day of the attack. All the guns in the valley opened fire, all the guns on the high plateau behind us, this time it was our bombardment, not his. It was too dark to see anything, but some time later I climbed to the top of the terraced banks behind our guns and looked across the valley to the rising ground on the other side. Through the smoke and semi-darkness I saw a line of tanks ascending the hill, and infantry following. I could see the red flashes of our own shells bursting along the ridge beyond the tanks, beyond the village of Hamel, which seemed already to have been captured. I saw no Germans.

You don't see very much of a battle when you are taking part in it. In March I had seen lines of German infantry coming downhill at a run, now I saw tanks going up a hill and our men walking quite slowly behind them. That was all I saw of two battles. It's much better on TV or at the cinema, the battles there look far more realistic.

Only a few shells came back at us. All the signs were that the attack was succeeding. Later in the morning Cherry gave us the official report: All objectives captured and 1,500 prisoners, our casualties not heavy. Some Australians passing by on the road gave us more details of the victory, the Yanks had fought very well, they said, they were fine soldiers, but a bit rough.

That evening we were taken out of the line, we were to march through the night to St Sauveur, nearly twenty miles from Vaux, in the valley of the Somme, but on the other side, the safe side, of Amiens. But that was to be only a temporary stopping place.

It looked like Rest, Cherry said; and not before it was time. We had been in the line for months and months and months. This was the best time of year for going out to rest,

I was thinking, as we marched through the warm summer night; long days, and the cleanness of the country away from the smells and the sultry heat in the battle zone. We were tired, but rest would restore us, make us ourselves again, a happy battery, working together. We might even go back as far as the sea, it was not a great distance from St Sauveur. The thought of bathing in the sea went to my head. The Somme lake had been enjoyable, but the Sea!

In the morning, after daylight, we saw Hughes coming to meet us. He had been sent on ahead to arrange about billets in St Sauveur, we were nearly there now. It was clear that he had heard news.

'Is it the sea?' we called out to him. 'Where are we going?'

'Y-prez,' he said, 'bloody Y-prez.'

Eight

So Flanders was our destination.

Jack said it was like going home. The Somme gave him the creeps, he said, he could see a picture of his corpse lying out on one of those ruddy bare hillsides; Ypres was at any rate a more cosy place to be killed in.

The rest of us laughed at the thought of Jack seeing a picture of his own corpse. 'Well, it's going to be our turn one of these days, whether we like it or not,' he said. He might feel pleased at going back to Flanders, but the rest of us were not; and when the train was carrying us along by the sea, so near to England, so infinitely far away, it was almost more than I could bear, and I saw some of the men turning their faces away.

My own depression had been gradually lifting. Peaceful days and nights at the wagon lines, bathing in the lake, the Australian successes, even the mere passing of time all these were helping me to forget the nightmares of March and April, I was more relaxed, less nervous about the morrow as I was falling asleep, able to make plans about the next day. And the year was half over. If we could hold out until it ended, then the Americans would be ready and the tide would begin to turn.

But all my depression came back when we arrived in Flanders.

We learnt at once that the next German attack was now expected up here. Not on the Somme. That was why we had been brought up. The battery was in action in what had been wagon line country in 1917, there were deserted camps all round us. But as a result of the enemy advance in April it was now in the fighting area, all the surrounding country was

80

dominated by Kemmel Hill, which the Germans had captured. There was no getting away from Kemmel Hill, wherever we went we could see it. And it could see us. I had never disliked a hill so much, it looked so menacing. It was Kemmel that first brought back my depression.

Two guns were in front of the others, a forward section again. They were behind the Scherpenberg, another wooded hill, like Kemmel but not so high, and not dominating the enemy positions as Kemmel dominated ours. The guns were side by side on the concrete floor of an old stable, part of one of the derelict camps. There was a tin roof overhead and a strip of camouflage netting along the open side, which had to be taken down when the guns fired. But no firing was done by day, the position was too close to the line, about a mile away.

There was no protection by the guns, but a house some fifty yards away had been converted into dug-outs. There were three of them, all strong. The dug-outs were all right, it was the thought of having to leave them and run across to the guns under fire when the attack came—that was the frightening thought. I was in charge of the forward section.

It was a sinister place. Jack said that the Somme gave him the creeps, this lonely derelict country behind the Scherpenberg had the same effect upon me. Once it had been attractive country, the Scherpenberg had been a pretty hill. Now it was a waste land, rough grass, a few forlorn huts, shell-holes; all the trees on the hill, which was just inside our line, were fleshless skeletons.

Since no firing was done by day I did not have to stay at the forward section. I spent the night there, returning to the main position in time for lunch and going up again in the evening. 'The attack is expected tomorrow,' I was told one day as soon as I rejoined the others. Major Cecil described the situation to me. The line was not being held in strength, he said, a withdrawal was intended; my two guns were to be sacrificed, I was to go on firing them for as long as possible, then to blow them up, no attempt would be made to save them, it would be impossible to get teams up during an attack.

This was even worse than I had feared. I had not expected

81

to be left on my own responsibility, to have to make all the decisions myself, including the hardest one—the right moment for blowing up the guns.

'It looks as though you will be on your own from the moment the show starts,' Major Cecil said.

I spent the afternoon reading all the orders. There seemed no doubt about the attack; prisoners had given the date, our airmen had reported the arrival of trains at all the railheads and seen the roads behind the line packed with men and transport moving up. It was a repetition of what we had been told on the eve of March 21st, I had made fun of it then, but it had been true.

I read with especial care the orders that concerned myself and my forward guns: . . . to go on firing for as long as possible . . . open sights . . . inflicting heavy casualties . . . holding up the enemy advance . . . then destroying the guns . . . ensuring their complete destruction . . . afterwards rejoining the rest of the battery.

Rejoining the rest of the battery! What a hope! We should all be killed before we got away. If we carried out those orders!

I should have felt less discouraged if we had still been behind the Australians, but the English division holding the line on our front seemed to consist only of young soldiers straight from home with no battle experience. How could they stand up to an attack like that of March 21st! Would they run away? Or would they wait to be taken prisoner? I might see them coming back over the skyline, or I might see no one at all until I saw the enemy.

And another thing. It would have been less difficult for me if the men up with the forward guns had been from my own Left Section; if Sergeant Denmark had been with me, he would have done what I told him to do, and I would have done what he told me to do, I had complete confidence in him. But they were not my own men, and Sergeant Tweedie was not reliable. On the surface he was more respectful than Denmark, but when we were in a tight corner he might be the first to disappear.

I went up earlier than usual. Jack wished me luck as I was leaving. I knew I should need it. I sent for Sergeant Tweedie

82

as soon as I arrived at the forward position and told him about the expected attack and what was required of us. He showed no concern whatever.

'Then we've got to be ready to blow up the guns, Sir,' he said, and he fetched two shells, unscrewing their cases. I watched him carefully. I had a vague idea as to what had to be done, but blowing up guns was not one of the things we had been taught at cadet school. He made sure that the caseless shells fitted easily, point inwards, into the mouth of the guns, then took them out again and put them on one side.

'Then you put another shell in the breech in the ordinary way, Sir, and fire.'

It sounded very simple.

'You need a longish bit of wire to tie to the trigger, Sir, and it's best to get round a corner before you pull.'

He went away to find some wire. He might be all right in the morning, I thought, no one could have set about the preparations in a more matter-of-fact way. The barrels of the guns would be completely destroyed by the explosion of the two shells inside. Major Cecil was said not to have destroyed his guns effectively on the first day of our retreat, that was the basis of the charge against him, the reason for his demotion.

Tweedie came back with the wire and hung the pieces over a nail on one of the stable beams.

'I'll see the lads know where they are,' he said. 'Will that be all, Sir?'

I gave him the details for our nightly harassing fire. It would be especially important tonight, for the enemy would be moving up to his assault line in the darkness, and short sudden bursts of fire might inflict a lot of casualties on him.

Then Tweedie went back to the dug-outs, but I remained standing by the guns. The light was beginning to fade, but I could still see all the ground in front rising to the Scherpenberg, and we had taken down the camouflage netting at the side of the stable in preparation for our night firing.

I could make some of my decisions now, I thought, while it was light enough to see. The enemy bombardment would probably start at about four o'clock, before daylight, the sun rose at five. It was certain to be very heavy, and nothing would be gained by bringing the men outside in the dark. But as soon as it was light we ought to come out. But we should have no protection inside the stable, we shouldn't last long here under heavy shellfire. It might be better to stay inside the dugouts until the shellfire was less heavy, the enemy would have to stop shelling the forward area as soon as his infantry began to advance, that would be the time when we could inflict most casualties.

Yes, that would be best. Wait inside under cover until the shellfire became less. That would tell us he was coming. Then we would rush out and wait until we saw him. The more I thought about it, the clearer it was to me that our job was to fire at him at short range. Other batteries could fire at him in his front line before he attacked, but ours were the only guns in a position to fire at him over open sights as he was attacking, as he came down the side of the Scherpenberg.

But how long could we go on for? I had never fired over open sights, I did not know of anyone who had, not at short range. It was little more than a thousand yards to the crest of the hill, we should come under rifle and machine-gun fire almost immediately. We should get cover from sight, perhaps even from bullets, behind the gun-shields, but anyone walking about inside the stable or carrying ammunition to the guns would be seen and shot at. And if our own infantry were falling back in front of the enemy we should have to wait until they were out of danger, probably it would be too risky to fire at a range of less than a thousand yards, but we could fire as the enemy was coming over the crest, and go on firing. The crest was the place. I would get both guns laid on to it as soon as we came out in the morning.

But I should have to watch the enemy's advance, see how far he was getting. With all these huts about, he might work his way round behind us and then rush the stable. I put up my field glasses for a last look at the country in front, I looked at the crest, moving my eyes along it, wondering where he was most likely to appear first, then at the deserted broken huts, finally choosing one of them, half way up to the crest. When I saw an enemy there or at any point in line with it, then I would give the order to blow up.

Some of the men with me were very good, young Gunner

Dee was first-rate. Whatever he might be doing he always had a cigarette between his lips and a mocking remark ready to come out of them, usually at the expense of one of us or a senior N.C.O., but spoken so quietly and with such a friendly smile that even Major Cecil did not take offence. Dee would be all right, smoking and mocking as he fired his gun, he was a first-rate gunner too, but some of the others were new men and Sergeant Tweedie was unlikely to set a good example. I could imagine him coming to me, I could hear him saying Better go, Sir, while we can. . . . We can get new guns, Sir, we can't get new men. . . . Probably he would bring me the bits of wire ostentatiously—If we wait too long, Sir, there won't be time.

It was nearly dark now, too dark to see. I went back to my dug-out, the smallest of the three, there was just room in it for my wire-netting bed and an empty ammunition box which served as a table.

Presently I heard our ammunition wagons on the road and we all went outside to unload them and carry the shells into the stable. I enjoyed talking to the drivers, but when they had gone back, when the last sound of horses and wagon wheels had died away I felt we had been deserted, they were returning to the safety of the wagon lines, we were waiting for the enemy to come, day would break as usual for them. But for us?

Three or four times more we went outside for the night firing. The last burst of fire was finished soon after two o'clock. Two hours to wait! This would be the hardest time. The men's dug-outs were very close to my own, I could hear their voices, but only an occasional word of what they were saying. They were playing cards, I heard a lot of laughter. I wanted to go and be with them, generally when I was alone on a job I would spend a part of the night at any rate in their company. They would move up when I went in, making room for me to sit down among them, but then go on with whatever they were doing, as though I was not there.

But tonight I thought it would be a mistake to go to them. It might make it harder for me in the morning, harder to get their obedience when I ordered them out, ordered them to go on firing. If I had been on equal terms with them an hour or

85

two before, they might not appreciate the difference when I had to be an officer again. I had never ordered men to risk their lives in this way, and go on risking them. Young Dee would carry out his orders, and perhaps the others would follow his example, they all liked him. I had a sudden idea, I would recommend him for the Military Medal if we both survived the attack, he certainly deserved one.

Three o'clock. I was trying to read my book, but I did not take in what I was reading. Instead of words on the page, I saw Germans, Germans coming over the crest, lines of Germans advancing down the hill, single Germans crouching behind the derelict huts. The card players were still at their game. Once, in a silence, I heard Dee's voice and then general laughter. Who was he mocking or mimicking now, I wondered. Myself perhaps, they must all have noticed my nervousness when we went outside for the night firing, for each time I had made sure that the two caseless shells and the bits of wire were still in their right places.

Half past three. I thought of writing a letter to my parents to thank them for the happy life they had given me. But it was too late now, there was no one to whom I could give my letter, it would never be delivered. Anyway, I could not have written, I was listening all the time for the first sound of the German guns, the opening of the bombardment. I should not have known what I was writing. Better to do nothing. Just keep still.

Four o'clock. The card-playing had stopped, there was no sound from the other dug-outs, they had all fallen asleep. It would not matter, the bombardment would waken them.

A quarter past. I had taken my watch out of my pocket and put it on the table in front of me. The candle, stuck into an empty bottle, had nearly burnt down, I lit another and put it on top of the old one, watching the shadows flicker on the sandbagged walls as I did so.

Half past four. Any moment now. All my senses were alert. I looked at the map again, making some notes on it about enemy trench mortar positions that had been reported. This was something to do, it helped to pass the time away. Silence still outside. He was late. It must be getting lighter, but the gas blanket was drawn so closely across the entrance that no light could come through. I felt tired, it had suddenly come over me.

Five o'clock. Hope began to rise. I could see the minute hand of my watch moving.

Five minutes past.

Ten past.

I waited, holding my breath, for the minute hand to reach the quarter. Then I got up, drew aside the blanket, and went out. The sun was up, it was over the crest, above the place where I had expected to see Germans by this time. And a lark was singing above the waste fields. Even the sad flat Flanders landscape looked beautiful in the light of a new day. A safe day. There would be no attack now. It must have been postponed for some reason. Tomorrow instead, probably. But a day was a long time. Twenty-four hours. Fourteen hundred and forty minutes.

I went back into the dug-out, blew out the candle, and fell asleep without undressing.

Nine

The German attack was never made.

It had been intended, it was not a hoax. At the time we did not know why it had been postponed, we knew nothing of Ludendorff's difficulties, nor did we want to know the reason; it was enough for us that it had been put off and that there was no immediate talk of its being put on again. We did not know that the tide was turning, had already turned in fact. Neither did Ludendorff.

We did not stay in Flanders. We were sent back to the Somme country as soon as it became apparent that the German attack was off. Again we were hoping for a fortnight's rest before returning to the line. 'Then we'll get you off on leave,' Cherry said to me encouragingly, I was next but one on the list. Again we were disappointed. We learnt as soon as we were out of the train that it was Villers Bretonneux again for us, the little town on the high ground above the river. And at once. We had at least been given one day's rest at St Sauveur on the way up, now we were to begin our march back to the line that very night.

The Battery was in a bad state. Our casualties had been very slight in Flanders, they had not been heavy at any time during the summer, far less than at Ypres the year before, but I had never heard so much grumbling. Chiefly it was the result of war weariness, the War had lasted so long, it would go on for ever and ever, there had been no leave since the beginning of the Retreat, there was nothing to look forward to.

But Major Cecil was responsible for some of the discontent. He was an unpopular battery commander. He had a sarcastic tongue, he wanted everything to be done in his way, he made no effort to cultivate a friendly relationship with the men under his command, the affection of his dog seemed to be enough for him.

'When's the Major coming back?' was a question I had often been asked during the summer. When they spoke of the Major the men meant Major Eric, who had gone home with a broken knee-cap at the beginning of the year. He had been as popular in the battery as Cecil was unpopular. He had been far more abusive than Cecil ever was, I had often heard him blasting someone or other, but the men had not minded. 'The Major, he plays hell with us when he's in a bad temper,' his servant, Hewlett, said to me once, 'but no one minds what he says, he wouldn't hurt a fly.'

Major Eric was a Sheffield man, a lot of the battery had known him before the War, they knew his family, they considered it right that he should command them, it was almost a feudal relationship; and in return the Major talked to them about their homes, he understood them, they knew that he took a personal interest in them.

But Major Cecil was without the gift of making himself liked. He was almost equally unpopular with the officers. I had a row with him on the morning of our return to the Somme. It had begun to rain while we were detraining, everyone was wet and in a bad temper, we marched a mile or two, then halted in a wet field, where we were to stay until nightfall. There was a house for us in the village and I went there, hoping to find a fire where I could dry my clothes. Major Cecil was there already. He told me his servant had been put on to some job, getting firewood or peeling potatoes, but he had taken him off it. 'His job is to look after me,' he said. 'Someone else can peel the potatoes.'

I was mess secretary, that was why he told me. I said that all the servants ought to take their share of whatever had to be done, it would not be fair if one of them did nothing.

'Fair or unfair, those are my orders,' he said. 'Tell Bombardier Medley that it's not to happen again.'

'You can damned well tell him yourself,' I said.

He told me I was getting too big for my boots, and I slammed out of the house, out into the rain again, back to the wet horse lines in the wet field, where the men were putting up their wet bivvies. They were all bad-tempered, and I agreed with them that it was a bloody awful war.

For the rest of the day I kept out of Cecil's way. After dinner he rode on ahead. 'To make sure of a good night's rest,' I said to the others, but I knew that in fact he was going to a conference of battery commanders with the Colonel. But he would be able to go to bed when it was over, none of the rest of us had any sleep that night. Frank to my annoyance took his side in the argument about the servants. Now that he was a senior officer himself he said their servants had more to do, and that Medley ought to have made a different arrangement. But Jack and Durham agreed with me, Hughes was on a course, he had been away from the battery during most of our time in Flanders.

'Don't worry,' said Jack sympathetically. 'It doesn't matter and there's nothing you can do about it.'

'Yes there is,' I told him. 'I can apply for a transfer to the R.A.F. or the Heavies.'

'No you can't,' said Durham. 'You've got to stay here, we need you.'

I was taken aback. It was as unexpected as it was comforting to be told that I was needed. I knew that I should not really choose to leave the battery.

We began our march at eleven o'clock that night. Some of the men were drunk when it was time to start, they had been to the estaminets in the village and they were not accustomed to wine. I was dismayed, it was further proof that the battery I loved was going downhill. Sergeant Denmark was completely sober, but he was in one of his bolshevik moods when I commented about our bad start and the fact that one of the other sergeants had obviously drunk too much.

'The officers have their good time when they get the chance,' he said. 'I reckon we have a right to do the same.'

I might have replied that we did not get drunk when there was a job to be done, but I remembered that we had dined in a restaurant on the previous evening before our train left, and that he had probably heard our loud voices when we returned to the station.

The men soon marched themselves sober. Long before daybreak I heard their cheerful ribald comments going up and down the line of our marching column. It was seven o'clock before we reached our destination and we were still on the near side of Amiens. It had kept fine during the night, but the rain soon started again. There was a lot to be done, we all got wet through once more. At lunch time Major Cecil told me that Medley needed keeping up to the mark, the servants had a soft job, he said, and if they didn't watch out he would return the whole lot to duty, there were plenty of other men who would be glad to take their places.

I did not tell Bombardier Medley about these threats, but he knew that Cecil had been finding fault again and he told me that he wanted to return to duty. 'I've had about as much as I can stand,' he said. 'If he thinks we've got cushy jobs, let him try and get someone else. We all want to go back. All except Richards, he can do the whole flicking lot by himself and find out what it's like."

Richards was Cecil's own servant, a decent young man, but in danger of being spoiled by Cecil's treatment of him. I calmed Medley down. We could not possibly do without him, he was not only a good cook, but a brave man who made sure that we got our meals whatever the Boche was doing.

I got two or three hours sleep during the afternoon, but we were to march again as soon as it was dark. The guns were to be taken away for calibration, Durham was going with them, the rest of the battery was to continue its march up to the line, through Amiens, I was to go on ahead with half a dozen guides, leaving one at each of the last turnings. We had got to arrive in our wagon line area before dawn, Cecil said. What was all the hurry about, why all this night marching?

I set off with my guides before the rest of the battery. We made quite a cavalcade, for there was a similar party from each of the other batteries and Major Villiers, the brigade second-in-command, was leading us. It was not yet midnight when we came to the outskirts of Amiens. Hardly anyone was left in the big town, the enemy was only nine miles away, the place was within gun-fire range. Not a great deal of damage had been done yet, in the darkness none was visible, but this added to the unnaturalness of our ride through the town. This great city and no one living in it! Once or twice a figure scurried across the road in front of us, and I saw an old woman behind a wall of sandbags. All was in darkness. I was aware of big houses and walled gardens, or broad streets and tram lines, boarded-up shops, the dark mass of the cathedral. It might have been a plague town, from which all the inhabitants had fled.

At last we came out on the other side. The noises of war were louder now and the sky in front of us was lit up by the flashes of guns. Still we rode on. We had turned away from the river valley, we were going uphill, I could see banks by the side of the road and little woods; it was the old familiar upland country, but now we were on the south of the Somme, we had been on the north side before we went up to Flanders.

I was riding beside Vernon, my friend in B Battery. I had not seen him for two or three weeks, the other batteries had not been near us in Flanders. He told me that he had applied for three months special leave to South Africa, where his home was now, he had not seen his parents for three years. I said I hoped he would get it, but I was almost selfish enough to hope that he would not. Three months was a long time, he would be away for nearly six altogether, I could not envisage a time so far ahead, I might never see him again, I hated the thought of losing another friend.

'I shall come back of course,' he said.

I knew he would. Some people seized with both hands any opportunity of escaping from the War, but not Vernon, I knew that he meant what he said. But I might not be here when he came back. I wanted to tell him about my row with Major Cecil and that I was thinking of applying for a transfer. He also had suffered from Cecil and I knew he would be sympathetic but would advise me to stay where I was, which was the advice I wanted. But after passing through Amiens I was too tired to talk, it was our third night without sleep. We spoke less and less, we were falling asleep.

'Look out!' he suddenly cried, bumping his horse against mine and catching hold of my shoulder. 'You were nearly off that time,' he said.

I tried to wake myself up, but the desire for sleep was almost irresistible.

'You drowse for ten minutes,' he said. 'I'll see you don't fall off. Then you can watch for me.'

So we went on. It was the darkest hour before the dawn.

At last we stopped. We had left the road, we were on a grassy track, I could see a big wood in front of us. We tied up our horses and lay down on the grass.

I was awakened by a shout: 'The batteries are here,' and looking down the track I saw them coming towards us. Day was breaking, I was shivering with cold, Vernon led his battery into one part of the wood, I guided ours to another. I saw the tired faces of the men as they dismounted, hardly anyone spoke, even during the Retreat we had not been more exhausted. The wagons were parked, horse lines put up, everyone working mechanically. Walkenshaw brought me a cup of very strong tea and showed me where he had unrolled my valise on the ground. I was asleep in a few minutes.

I woke up once and heard the voice of Hughes. So he had come back from his course. 'Hello!' he said, seeing my eyes open. His cheerful smiling face was wet with sweat. 'Coo!' he said. 'Known it colder than this in December." But I could not wake up, or say how pleased I was to see him. When I woke again it was the middle of the afternoon. My head ached, the wood was full of horses and shouting men. And smells and flies, there were flies buzzing everywhere.

'No one is to go out of the wood by day.' Major Cecil said when we were all together at tea. The servants had done a good job, they had put up the mess and all our little tents.

Why ever not, we all wanted to know.

We were going to attack, and the Boche was not to find out that a lot of fresh troops had come into the area. The guns were not to go up until the night before the attack, or to fire at all before zero hour. It was hoped that we should take him by surprise.

So that was the reason for all our night marching, and why the guns had been taken away for calibration. The normal thing to do was to check their accuracy by observed firing whenever we went to a new position, but on this occasion we were not to give our position away until the battle started.

'What about the horses?' Frank asked. 'Are they to stay inside the wood all day?'

There was no water in the wood. The horses would have to go all the way to Boves, more than a mile away, three times a day. It was absurd to suppose that Boche aeroplanes would never see them, it was absurd to think we could deceive the Boche, he always knew what we were going to do, he would be ready for us. But it was rather exciting, after he had been attacking us for so long. Even an unsuccessful attack of ours might be less disagreeable than a successful attack of his.

My head was still aching the next day. In the afternoon I rode up to the line with Jack to see the position we were going to occupy. It was behind Villers Bretonneux, only a thousand yards from the enemy, but we rode all the way because it was raining and there was no visibility. The afternoon was quiet, there were not many shell-holes on the position, we agreed that the place might have been worse. There was also a shallow trench close behind, Hughes was going up with a working party that night to make it deeper and dig some shelters.

We were both soaked when we got back to the wood. It had been fine when we set off and because it was so hot we had not taken our coats. Then the storm broke. There was so much water in my boots when I took them off that I could pour it out. With any luck, I thought, I'll get pneumonia or rheumatic fever. That would do as well as applying for a transfer.

By this time I was beginning to enjoy my row with Major Cecil, I had not spoken to him since our arrival in Boves Wood, but one of the others told him about my headache and to my disappointment he was considerate. 'You've had a harder time than anyone else lately,' he said to me, 'I shall leave you behind at the wagon lines when the guns go up.'

I should have preferred to go up with the guns, I felt part of the battery when I was there, but only a supernumerary at the wagon lines; but I was not feeling well, I wanted to sleep and go on sleeping, and there was more time for sleep at the wagon lines. But there was so much noise in the wood. It was full of horses and men, full of Canadians, who were going to make the attack on our front. Wherever you went there was a latrine and the wood was deep in horse dung, the place was a paradise for flies, in the August heat and the mud after the rain.

In the morning, however, I felt better. The guns were going up that night, the attack was to take place the next morning. Orders had been received that we were to be ready to travel light, everything inessential was to be left behind, to be dumped in the rear if necessary. The others were all wondering what they should take and what they should leave behind, but not being concerned in this, since I was remaining at the wagon lines, I rode off after breakfast to draw money from the Field Cashier and look for canteens.

I enjoyed my ride, I always enjoyed seeing and learning my way about in new country. It was a satisfaction to feel well again and to escape even for a few hours from the smells in the wood. I went alone. I saw Edric coming to meet me on my return. There was a particular smile on his face, not his ordinary smile of welcome, it meant that he had news.

"Major's come back," he said.

"What major?" I asked, but of course I knew who he meant. Major Eric. I was amazed. The news was rippling over the wood, three other men told me before I reached the mess.

There he was. Sitting the wrong way round on his chair, resting his arms on the back of it, his cap on the back of his head, the buttons of his tunic undone, a glass on the table beside him; it was as though he had never gone away. He smiled at the look of astonishment on my face. Everyone was laughing. Even Major Cecil seemed pleased to see him, they were old friends. But what was going to happen now? We could not have two majors in one battery. Would Cecil become a captain again, and Frank a lieutenant? We had always said to one another that if he ever came back he would turn up in this way without any warning, but we had not expected that he would come back.

'You can't get rid of a bad penny,' he said.

He was enjoying our surprise and our pleasure in seeing him. But why hadn't he come back before, a broken knee cap need not have kept him in England for six months. He knew all about us. Who had told him? No one had written to him, so far as I knew, he himself never wrote a letter. But he knew all the places where we had been and who had been killed and who wounded, he even knew about Bingley's revolver.

'Nice chap, but out of his element,' he said. 'Like a fish out of water.'

He did most of the talking at lunch. He told us he had read *The Times* from cover to cover during the March Retreat.

'I was expecting to see some familiar names in the list of Victoria Cross winners,' he said.

'What a hope you had!' said Frank. 'It was terrible. We did everything that we should not have done and nothing that we should have done. We ran away more than once. The other batteries were worse, that's all we can boast about."

I felt rather sorry for Cecil at this reference to the other batteries, but he said nothing, and Major Eric went on, 'Sergeant Denmark was the man in my mind, I knew no Fritz could frighten him, I imagined him firing his gun at point-blank range.'

'He was on leave,' I said.

'So he has just told me.'

He knew all about us, but he told us nothing about himself, where he had been, what he had been doing, why he had come back at last. Frank told us, Jack and myself, later in the day that he knew all about it. His woman had left him, he said, she had taken up with another man. That was why he had come back.

'How do you know all this?' Jack asked.

'Everyone in Yorkshire knows about her, she's notorious,' Frank said. 'And the sooner Eric stops running after her, the better for him. I know he's got a lot of money, but not enough for the like of her.'

Frank enjoyed having a story to tell, but he may have been right. I thought the Major seemed different after his return. He was quieter, he drank as much as before, but he was less hospitable, he was not always inviting other officers into our mess. Not many of his friends in the brigade were left, and he did not appear to want to make new ones. He enjoyed talking to the men as much as before, at any rate to the old Yorkshire ones, they made less than half the battery now. He preferred their company to ours, none of us could come as close to him as they did.

They were delighted at his return. 'Now our luck will change, Sir, you just see,' old Driver Oaks said to me, and he added, 'the Major, he buggers us about, but we'd rather be buggered about by him than by any of the others."

The guns went up to the line that night. Major Cecil went with them. Major Eric stayed behind at the wagon lines with Frank and myself. 'You don't swop horses in mid-stream,' he said.

We were about to attack. It was our turn now.

Ten

August

Up at the guns Zero Hour was at twenty minutes past four, down at the wagon lines I was wakened by the bombardment. I got up and looked out of my tent, it was quite dark in the wood and there was a thick mist. What was happening up there! But it was easy to imagine the scene, I had been there so often—all the German rockets, calling for help, their guns replying, the fountains of earth leaping up where each shell burst; and the thunder of our own guns, it was almost impossible to hear yourself speak on the morning of a battle. We were probably having a bad time, I thought, being so close to the line. I tried to distinguish the sound of enemy shells bursting from the cannonade of our own guns, but Boves Wood was a long way back, and at a distance it was all one noise, a sullen ceaseless reverberation. The drums of death.

For once I was not directly concerned, I was in safety at the wagon lines, I could go back to sleep for another hour. The morning mist was cold, and it was a physical pleasure to feel the warmth of my sleeping bag when I got back inside it.

When I woke again the noise had almost stopped and this was surprising, battles lasted for more than an hour or two, whether we won or lost. The silence was rather disconcerting, I could interpret noises, but silence, even this comparative silence, was a new feature in a battle. There was no news yet. The wagon lines were to move at nine o'clock, unless the order was cancelled before that time.

Taking the horses down to water in the river at Boves I felt a proper wagon-line hero, it was the first time I had not been with the guns on the day of a battle. From Boves I could see the enemy observation balloons against the sky, looking no further away than usual. If the attack had been successful they would have been forced to go further back. We hated these sausage balloons, they could watch everything we were doing.

But no cancellation order was received and we got away from the wood at the right time. It was much emptier now, the Canadians had gone up the night before, they were attacking on the right, the Australians in the centre, and British troops on the left, across the Somme. The roads were blocked, at first we moved very slowly, but there was no enemy shellfire. That was a good sign. Then we saw prisoners coming back, a lot of them. Another good sign. But still there were those damned balloons watching us. They must be able to see all the wagons and lorries on the road. Why weren't we being shelled! What was the matter with his guns!

Then an extraordinary idea occurred to me. Could they be our balloons, not his! Could the attack have been so successful that our balloons were already up there, where his had been only yesterday?

I was riding at the rear of our column, now I went quickly up to the front to tell Frank and the Major about my extraordinary idea. They nodded their heads in agreement. Frank was looking very pleased.

'If everything's gone according to plan,' the Major said, 'we shan't know what to do.' He told me to ride on ahead to the guns and to find out whether it was all right for the rest of the battery to come up. I galloped away. It was unbelievable, nothing like this had ever happened before.

I saw Hughes and Durham standing by the guns and I shouted to them, 'What's happened? Who's winning?'

'We are,' said Durham. 'Forty-love.'

'Jerry's on his way back to Berlin,' Hughes said.

Jack had seen me coming and now he joined us. Even he was smiling. 'I can't make head or tail of it,' he said.

I sent Edric back with a message for the Major, telling him it was all right to come on. Then I got off my horse and listened to what they had to tell me. They all talked at the same time.

'Fairly caught him napping this time,' said Hughes.

'It was bad to begin with,' said Jack.

'Oh, it was nothing. Half a dozen pip-squeaks!' said Durham.

'Well, we had three or four men hit.'

'Could hardly see the tanks because of the fog.'

'You ought to have seen the cavalry going past.'

'Cavalry?' I said in amazement. 'Cavalry?'

'You know,' Durham said impatiently. 'Soldiers on horseback.'

Cavalry coming up from the seaside, where they had been living for years, and going into action! I could not take in such an extraordinary feature of a battle.

They told me they had seen a lot of prisoners and that Major Cecil had invited some of the officers into the mess and given them a drink. One of them spoke good English and he admitted that the attack had taken them completely by surprise.

'But he was still confident of a German victory,' Jack said.

Durham made a contemptuous noise. 'He'll change his mind,' he said, 'when he sees how full the cage is.'

Hughes was rather indignant at Cecil's hospitality. 'Wonder how many of our poor fellows were given a drink in March,' he said. But the others had enjoyed seeing and hearing the German officers.

'What's going to happen now?' I asked. We had been expecting to go forward if the attack was successful, that was why the teams and wagons had been ordered to come up. But they did not know, they only knew that there were no Boche within miles, the guns had stopped firing hours ago because there was no enemy within range.

'It's a shame that we're missing all the fun,' Durham said.

'He'll counter-attack,' said Jack, 'he'll get it all back. Like he did at Cambrai last year.'

We were not sent forward, we stayed in corps reserve in case of a counter-attack. We moved two or three miles during the afternoon, but to a flank, southwards, away from Villers Bretonneux. In the evening I took the horses to water in the little river Luce, we crossed no-man's-land, we went inside what had been enemy land in the morning. His front-line trench was full of bodies, all Germans, they were the first dead Germans I had seen for a long time, I had never seen so many in one place. The sight of them gave me no elation, as once it would have done. Satisfaction yes, we had won a great and totally unexpected victory; but elation no. In March our front-line trench must have looked like that, full of brave Jocks and South Africans.

It was a beautiful summer evening, and the little river Luce was beautiful. It was like a little river in England and the flowers growing at the water's edge, where my horses were drinking, were English flowers. The water was so clean, the field in front of me looked utterly peaceful, but only fifty yards away there was that trench, full of dead Germans, we should see them again on our way back, the grey faces, the poor twisted bodies. They had been bayoneted by the Canadians in the morning, you can't take prisoners in a front-line trench in an attack. Wives, mothers, sweethearts, would not know yet, they would still be writing letters, but the letters would never be read. It might have been us.

I was glad that we were staying behind, but all the others said they were disappointed we had not followed up with the infantry. 'Might have found some of the things we lost in March,' Hughes said, and Frank said they gave army brigades all the dirty work to do, but left them out when it was easy. 'We've got to take the smooth with the rough,' the Major said.

It had already been arranged that he was to stay in command of our battery, Cecil had gone to A Battery in place of Major Villiers, who was unwell and about to go home. When he was leaving us we began to like Cecil again, we parted on the best of terms. I supposed I should never have anything more to do with him, but I was mistaken.

We were still in corps reserve the next morning, no counter-attack had been made. Some of us rode out to look at the scene of the fighting. Except in their front-line trenches there were not many German dead, our advance had been so rapid that most of the enemy had been surrounded and taken prisoner. And we did not see many of our own dead, but in one place there were twenty of our cavalry, men and horses lying where they had fallen, as some German machine-gunner perhaps had got on to them while they were galloping over the field.

There was a captured battery position, and half a dozen artillerymen were lying round one of the guns. Had they, I wondered, been firing over open sights at the Canadians or the cavalry as they came on! Should we have died as bravely that morning? It might have been us, on the stable floor behind the Scherpenberg. How could I feel elation!

We went into their dug-outs, they were strong and more comfortable than ours. Their guns were well concealed. In their officers' mess an unfinished meal, unwashed cups and plates were still on the table. Someone must have rushed in as they were eating, calling out 'The Tommies are here!' I did not know what they called us, we called them Jerry or Fritz or the Boche. *Time you got out, the Boche will be here in a few minutes.*

Their home was very like one of ours, maps and pictures stuck on the walls, shelves cut out of the earth, a sheaf of orders on a hook, newspapers on the table, a half-written letter, a pair of spectacles. I looked at their books, but I could not tell whether they were like ours, whether they were novels or not. Their pictures were certainly different. There was one of a German U-Boat arriving at Constantinople, I could tell it was Constantinople because of the domes and minarets, and sailors from the other ships in the harbour, waving at the submarine, were all wearing red fezzes. Fancy wanting to pin up a patriotic propaganda picture! We only had girls on the walls of our dug-outs, girls in underwear or in nothing at all. Jack had La Vie Parisienne sent to him and he allowed us to cut out what we liked.

He had come up beside me while I was looking at the picture. 'Not much of a thrill there,' he said.

The Major said they were nearer to their homes than we were and were given more leave. 'And you don't need picture thrills,' he said, 'when you can have the real thing.'

As I stood there, in the German officers' mess, looking at their pictures and their books and the little personal possessions that had meant so much to them, as ours meant to us, suddenly I was aware of a great weight being lifted from me. It was over, the nightmare was over, the nightmare that had begun in the spring and lasted all through the long midsummer months. I had woken up from my evil dream. It had

102

begun that morning in the fog. The smell of the wet fog came back to me, fog mixed with gas, I heard the menace of the German guns again, I saw the line of infantrymen on their way up, coming out of the fog, disappearing into it again almost at once. That had been the beginning of it, this was the end.

Not the end of fear or of danger, only the end of a nightmare. Tomorrow or the day after we should go back into the line, I might be killed, but I had always known this might happen and had accepted it, as any soldier must. What I had not known until it happened was the fear of defeat, of disgrace, of running away, of failure. That was worse than the fear of death, that was what had unnerved me.

Now in the German officers' dug-out, with the others round me, talking to one another and to me, comparing the way in which they did things with our way, as I stood there, taking part in their conversation, I knew that it was over. Whatever happened in the future I should never suffer the same fear again, I could feel that the weight had been lifted, I wanted to sing.

But my headaches came back. I thought I had left them in Boves Wood, but they returned. I wanted to sleep. We were still in corps reserve, there had been no counter-attack, but we moved back to Villers Bretonneux, our tents were in a corn field at the edge of the village, we stayed there for two days. I have no memory of them, I was asleep. I may have got up for meals and eaten them with the others, but I went back to sleep afterwards; I may have been woken by the German bombers, it was good bombing weather, moonlit nights, no wind, but I went to sleep again as soon as they had dropped their bombs; the others may have come into the tent where I was lying, I may have heard their voices, but they left me alone.

But at the end Durham came in and shook me gently. 'You'll have to wake up soon,' he said, 'we've got to move.'

'When?' I asked him.

'Tonight. You don't want to be left in corps reserve by yourself, do you?'

'No,' I said. 'I shall be ready.'

I asked him where we were going, but he did not know. 'Somewhere across the river,' he said. I knew that our attack had been less successful on the north side of the Somme. On our front the Canadians and Australians had gained all their objectives, it was the greatest victory we had ever won, but across the river we had not done so well, that was where the next battle would be.

We set off at dusk. It was goodbye to Villers Bretonneux, we never went there again. For myself it was goodbye to Amiens and the Somme and the Ancre also, to the lakes and wooded villages, to the high plateau between the rivers, and all the places where we had dug and laughed and been afraid during the summer.

We marched along the Roman road, the road to St Quentin, westwards, away from the War at first. The bombers were out again, and our road running straight, between dark woods, showed up like a silver ribbon in the moonlight. I knew another way, I had ridden all over this country in the summer, I told the Major we could leave the main road and go down into the valley, where we should be in shadow, I knew the way, we could cross the river by the same bridge, and from there it was easy.

So for a while I rode at the head of the column instead of in my usual place in the rear with the Left Section. It was just a week since we had been marching in the opposite direction, tired, dispirited, as men without hope. Now I was happy. My leave had been put off again, Frank had been given a compassionate leave because his brother had been killed, and I should have to wait at any rate until he came back; but I was happy. We were on our way to more fighting, and fighting meant wounds or death for some of us, it would be one battle after another, as it always had been; but I was happy. There was a sound of summer nights in the tops of the tall trees along the river valley. All was well.

'I told you our luck would change, Sir, when the Major came back,' Corporal Albert said to me after I had returned to my ordinary place. All the battery seemed to think that our great victory on August 8th had been won because the Major had come back to us on August 7th. He knew what the men were saying and accepted the position they gave him, but he had a way of making himself liked. 'Lucky, you knew that other road,' he said to me. 'I didn't fancy being stuck up there when those fellows were laying their eggs. Felt too damned conspicuous.'

It was four o'clock when we arrived at our destination, and still dark, but daylight had come before we went to our tents at the edge of a sweet-smelling clover field. Hughes woke me some hours later. He said he had found a pool in the little river near by, the Hallue, where we could swim one or two strokes. 'Anyway, it'll be cool,' he said, 'it's mighty hot here.

The water was very cold, for alder branches arched across the stream, shutting out the warmth of the sun, leaving only darting spots of light on its surface. Afterwards we lay naked in the hot sunshine.

'Feel the better for that,' Hughes said. 'Nothing like cold water for helping us keep our feelings under control.'

Hughes, the Welsh ex-policeman was a strong fine-looking man and at that moment, I thought, he would certainly have been an object of interest to the village girls we had seen on our way to the stream. But his girl was in Cardiff.

The clover field was only a pause on the way. Tomorrow we were to be off again, going forward this time, back into the battle area. In the evening Bombardier Ewell, the battery clerk, came into the mess tent with our orders from Brigade Headquarters. I saw a pink leave warrant among the other papers. Who was the lucky man, I wondered.

'A leave is no good to you, is it?' said the Major, looking in my direction. 'You haven't got a girl crying her eyes out for you.'

It appeared that an unexpected leave warrant had been allotted to the brigade, and the Colonel said that I might have it if Major Eric could spare two of his officers at the same time.

'Can we spare him?' the Major said. 'I don't think we can. What do you say, Ewell?'

Bombardier Ewell put on the polite smile that he reserved for an officer's pleasantry. He knew as well as I did that the Major would have spared every man in the battery to go on leave, or kept only one for himself to talk to. Ewell asked where I wanted to go, he had to fill in my destination on the railway warrant.

I could hardly believe it was real. The others were returning to the line, but I was going on leave tomorrow. England, I should see England again.

Eleven

September

There were two bad moments on every leave. There was the saying goodbye at home when it was over, and there was the moment of return to the battery when you looked to see, or waited to be told, if anyone was not there.

It took me a long time to find the battery on my return. I was travelling for four days in France, going backwards and forwards, from one place to another. No one seemed to know where the brigade was. That was one of the disadvantages of a small unit like an Army Field Artillery Brigade. We had stayed with the Australians for a long time, but as a rule we were attached to a different division two or three times every month, we were changed so often that sometimes we did not ourselves know what division we were with. We grumbled, we called ourselves Nobody's Children, but in fact we enjoyed our independence, we were less staff-ridden than divisional brigades.

I found the battery at last. We were out at rest, in a part of France I had never been to before, on the edge of the coal-mining country, we could see slag heaps in the distance. The others were having lunch when I arrived, but only the Major and Durham and a young officer called Allison, who had joined us during the summer. Where were the others? I knew Frank would not be there, he was getting married, he was certain to have applied for an extension of leave. But Hughes and Jack?

'It's all right,' Durham said. 'Jack's gone to Boulogne to buy a case of champagne for the mess, we thought we deserved one.'

'Where's Hughes?'

'He's all right too. A nice blighty, he'll be in England by this time.'

It was what everyone wanted, a wound that would take you home and keep you there for some months, so I felt pleased on his account, but I knew we should miss him. Someone had said, 'He isn't our sort,' when he first came to the battery. He wasn't, in the usual sense of the expression, but he was the sort we needed and I had often wished I was more like him.

The Major said his wound was a bad one. 'I thought at first he wasn't going to make it,' he said. 'I don't mind telling you we had a pretty sticky time while you were away.' Casualties had been heavier than at any time since the Retreat.

We stayed out at rest for most of September, but I was not altogether sorry when the time came for us to go back into the line. It had been very pleasant, we had enjoyed the summer sunshine, and having nothing to do, and sleeping all through the night; but we seemed to irritate one another more than when we were in the line. 'This sort of life's so unreal,' Jack said. 'The sooner we go back the sooner we shall settle down.'

We went back. On this occasion the change from peace to war was as sudden as it was complete. One evening we were so far from the War that we could not always hear it; the next, we were in the line and being bombed. It was nearly two months since I had been under fire, I had forgotten how very disagreeable it was, but the sound of falling bombs in the darkness close by was a wonderful aid to memory.

We were back in the Somme country. We were in fact only a few miles from Heudecourt, where our retreat had begun in March. All the territory lost in the spring had been regained in the last few weeks, and now we were back where we had started. The battery had detrained at Peronne in the afternoon, we had immediately marched up to the line and here we were, in the dark, in a maze of trenches and barbed wire, bombs dropping, and the teams and gun limbers still on the position.

'Home, sweet home!' said the Major, and he began humming unmelodiously 'Be it ever so humble,

There's no place like home.'

Humble it certainly was: an old tumbledown trench system, with some poky and uncomfortable shelters dug into the sides. But we were fortunate, none of us nor any of the horses were hurt by the bombs.

We were going to attack the Hindenburg Line, the name of the immensely strong defence system which the enemy had constructed at the time of an earlier retreat. We had attacked it the year before without any success. Now we were going to try again, but no one seemed to think we should do any better this time. Even the Australians said that we should find we were banging our heads against a stone wall.

We had taken over from an Australian battery, one of their officers had waited to hand over the position to us, and when our teams were safely away and the bombers had returned to their own homes he came into the mess, there was hardly room for four of us in the little excavation, and drank a bottle of whisky with the Major. Up to now, he said, everything had gone like clockwork, but the Hindenburg Line—well, he hoped his battery would not have to take part in the attack.

The Major said it was a bit late in the year to be attacking.

The Australian replied that he supposed the Staff had been waiting for the weather to break.

'I suppose Fritz knows all about it,' the Major said. 'We shan't surprise him this time.'

'He couldn't help knowing,' said the Aussie. 'We've been shouting it out.'

It was a discouraging start, and the next morning we were awakened before it was light by an S.O.S. alarm, and at once all the guns in the area began firing.

'It's only breeze,' the Major said. 'Someone's got a fit of the jumps. Fritz isn't going to attack us, he's sitting pretty, waiting for us to come over and be killed.'

The noise soon died down and as soon as it was light the Major said he was going to find out where we were. He took me with him.

'Christ! what a place!' he said when we saw it for the first time. Old trenches, barbed wire, shell-holes. There was nothing else to see in any direction, wherever we looked there were old trenches and barbed wire and shell-holes.

We walked for about half a mile, jumping over the trenches,

finding a way through the barbed wire, until we came to a trench full of Americans.

'Hello!' said the Major to them.

'Hello you!' they replied.

It was a surprise to learn that an American division, not an Australian one, was holding the line in front of us and that they had never been in action before. 'No wonder they had the jumps,' the Major said, as we were walking back. 'I should have had them myself if I'd known,' and he added that he could not see a new division with no battle experience cutting the Hindenburg Line into little bits.

But Cherry and the Colonel said we should find they were all right on the day, other American divisions had been fighting magnificently on the French front, and these fellows were longing to show us what they could do. Cherry said he knew we had already tried to break the Hindenburg Line and had not succeeded, but this time it would be altogether different, the old Boche was on the run, he had been in retreat ever since the beginning of August, he couldn't put the brake on now, all we had to do was to go on attacking, first in one place, then in another, that was the strategy now, we should go on driving him back until he reached his own country. It would be peace before Christmas, he said.

I had been studying the map of the country in front of us. The St Quentin Canal was part of the Hindenburg Line system, a wide stretch of water between steep banks. On our front, however, in front of the Americans, the canal went underground through a very long tunnel. This was where the Americans were to attack, and at first sight it looked easier to break through here then to cross the canal. But the enemy had made his preparations to meet the danger. The map showed one trench after another, and so many rolls of wire that it appeared impossible for any infantry to get through.

I had my first sight of the Hindenburg Line on the following day when I spent twenty-four hours at the O.P. It was a long walk up there, the O.P. was not directly in front of our battery position, but some little way to the south, on a ridge overlooking the canal itself, not the tunnel. I found my way there by following the telephone line, but it had not been used since our brigade took over, and the enemy knowing

110

about our forthcoming attack had been shelling the whole area, the line was broken in so many places that it would have been quicker to lay out a new one. Shellfire was still heavy, we often had to crouch on the ground, and as fast as we mended the line in one place it was broken in another, the line was still dead behind us when at last we reached the O.P., and in spite of all that my signallers could do it remained dead, I was never in communication with Brigade all the time I was there. I might as well have stayed at the battery for all the use I was.

But I saw the Hindenburg Line. I could see where the tunnel was, and where the canal came out of the tunnel by the village of Bellicourt, I could see the deep chasm of the canal between its steep banks, and the German trenches, white scars against the hillside. It was a very strong position. But most of all, it was the wire in front of the trenches that was disconcerting, there was so much and wire was so hard to destroy. It was our job to destroy it, the field gunners'. We had to cut it up using shells that burst on percussion without making much of a hole, heavier guns could have destroyed the wire more effectively, but if they made big craters in the ground, then it was difficult for the infantry to advance. We had already begun our shooting, it was to go on for forty-eight hours.

I could see the strength of the position, it was enough to daunt anyone. How could any troops cross that canal under heavy fire and scale the bank on the other side! An English division on our right was to make the attack opposite the canal, but it looked an impossible task. And how could the Americans get through that wire! They were to make the first advance at Zero Hour, the Australians following behind were then to go through them and make the second, but they would all be held up by the wire, it looked undamaged.

I could also see unspoiled country beyond the Hindenburg Line, undulating hills, villages, little woods, villages fit to live in, trees that bore leaves, a hillside without shell-holes. It was like a Promised Land. But it had not been promised to us, it would be ours only if we succeeded in storming the canal and capturing the trenches on the other side of the wire. If! Cherry had said we should succeed, but it was easy for an adjutant, planning battles but taking no part in them himself, it was easy for him to be optimistic. I hardly dared even to hope.

Yet I longed to walk on those green hills, hills on which no British soldier had ever set foot, to ride through those unspoiled villages, to hear the rain falling on leaves on living trees. It was an ache to be looking at those villages on the hill—Joncourt, Beaurevoir, Villers Outreaux. They looked so near, they were so far away. The Hindenburg Line stretched between us and them.

There was nothing for me to do except look at the country. Early the next morning I saw a German cart being driven along the road behind the canal, close up to the line, I could have shot at it if I had been in communication with the battery. The man was driving furiously, he knew his danger, he must have been delayed in some way and daylight had caught him, now he was galloping back towards safety, whipping up his horse. I was probably the only Englishman who saw him, and I could do nothing. But after one moment's regret at my impotence I felt sorry for him, I hoped he would escape, I was glad when he reached a bend in the road and was hidden from sight.

Then the rain began and the mist came down, and all the green unspoiled country was obliterated, only the white scars of the trenches remained, and the lines of wire, and the deep gash which was the canal.

At midday I was relieved by an officer in one of the other batteries and I started on my way back through the rain.

Almost at once I had a curious encounter. I met a man unlike anyone I had ever seen before in or near the line. He was old, forty at least, and was wearing a long and shabby mackintosh that reached almost to the ground. But it was his head-dress that gave him such a peculiar look. He was wearing a steel helmet, like anyone else, but he had covered it with an old woollen scarf, the ends of which were tied under his chin to protect his face from the rain.

I guessed that he must be a newspaper correspondent. I had never seen one before, but had formed a picture in my mind of what they probably looked like, and here was the picture come to life in front of me. They were not supposed to go off by themselves or to come so close to the line, but this old fellow had evidently escaped from his guards.

I felt sorry for him. He was too old to be out in the rain, and I thought he had the bewildered look that I had sometimes seen on the face of my father when he did not know where he was. I wanted to be nice to him. What they liked, I knew, war correspondents, was to be treated as equals by fighting men, so I talked to him as I would have talked to one of my friends, telling him about my 24 unrewarding hours at the O.P. and the unspoiled country I had seen across the canal. He asked my name and battery and about the part we were expecting to play in the forthcoming attack. I answered all his questions. Afterwards I wondered if I ought to have been so communicative in conversation with a man who was not a soldier; but I liked his face, as much of it as I could see between the flaps of his scarf, I was sure he was trustworthy. I even called him Sir once or twice, out of respect for his age and because of his resemblance to my father.

But I could not stay talking all day, I knew there was a job for me to do when I got back to the battery. So I told him I must go, and he said that he must also. To write up his dispatch, I supposed. I nearly asked him what his paper was, for I thought it would be amusing to get hold of a copy if I could and read about his meeting with a gay intrepid young observing officer—newspaper correspondents always wrote in that style. But I did not ask. If he had wanted me to know he would have told me. I felt of course the more experienced of the pair of us. He could not know anything about the real war, whereas by this time I thought I knew everything there was to be known about it.

I watched him till he was out of sight. I thought he might not realise how close he was to the German line, a wrong turning might lead him into it. So I watched, ready to run after him if he made a step in the wrong direction. Then I hurried on.

Jack was the senior subaltern in the gun line, but he was no good at working out a barrage table, lines of fire and ranges for our guns on the morning of an attack. That had always been Frank's task, but now that he had been promoted and was generally at the wagon lines it had become my responsibility. It needed complete concentration and great accuracy, but it was the kind of work I could do.

I was supremely confident of my ability to do it and of being able to explain to the Numbers One of each gun exactly what they must do.

It took me a long time. Getting up once, to stretch my legs, and looking outside I saw to my surprise that the Major now had been caught by my war correspondent. The Major was inclined to be intolerant and I was afraid he was probably being rude to the old gentleman. But he was following him about and seemed to be on his best behaviour.

'Who was that old fellow?' I asked when at last he came in for tea.

'Major-General Budworth, C.R.A. Fourth Army,' was the reply.

'Well, I'm damned!' I exclaimed.

'He told me he had met you,' the Major went on. 'He was quite complimentary, he said you were the kind of young officer the artillery would need after the war and hoped you were going to stay on in the army.'

I could not help feeling pleased. For once in my life I had made a good impression on a general, the highest-ranking general I had ever seen in the line.

At dusk we moved about a mile forward to our battle position, where Colonel Richardson and Cherry came to see us and to wish us luck for the next day. The news from all fronts was simply stupendous, Cherry said—the Bulgarians asking for peace, the Turks driven out of Palestine, the whole of the Western Front on the move. And tomorrow we should join in, it was going to be the biggest battle of the war and the greatest victory, he said; the Sammies were as good as the Aussies, together they would be irresistible, the Boche simply hadn't a chance.

'We shall go through them,' the Colonel said, 'like a knife through butter. We shall be eating our Christmas dinner in Berlin.'

They convinced me. I had seen with my own eyes that our task looked impossible, but their enthusiasm was so great that I was persuaded. That night I believed that we were about to enter the Promised Land I had seen from the O.P., I

114

should walk on those green hills where trees lived and villages were unspoiled. We were all equally confident, even Jack said there was just a chance of things going right.

But the morning was cold and unpromising when we went outside. Zero hour was at ten minutes to six. We opened fire, there was a great crash of artillery. Daylight came, but the fog was so thick that we could hardly see from one gun to the next. Someone said it was not natural fog, but an artificial one caused by our own smoke shells to help the infantry cross the canal and get through the wire. No one knew for certain. No one knew anything. In any case we didn't want a fog back here, we had to make an advance, how could we advance through this! Perhaps the wind had changed and was blowing the smoke back on ourselves.

'It doesn't smell like a victory,' Jack said.

But Frank found his way up with the gun limbers and first line wagons, we were to begin our advance at Z plus two hundred and forty.

'What's the news?' he asked.

Still there wasn't any. We had not seen any prisoners. Perhaps they had gone by in the fog without our seeing them.

We pulled the guns out. We began to advance. Along the Black Road. It was called a road, but the trenches had hardly been filled in and there were shell-holes everywhere. We advanced about half a mile. The fog was clearing, we could see other guns and wagons in front of us. They were not moving very fast. In fact they were not moving at all, we could not go on.

By this time we could see for four or five hundred yards, up to a crest in front. There were wagons and guns all the way up to the crest, but nothing was going over. Everyone knew what that meant, the enemy was still holding the Hindenburg Line, he would see us if we went over the crest.

Just then a gun began firing at us. There was only one gun and it wasn't a big one. But this was further proof that our attack had failed, a gun of this size only had a range of seven or eight thousand yards, indeed from the sound of the shells this one seemed only half that distance away. The place it was firing from ought to have been captured some hours ago.

Being under fire when mounted was always disagreeable,

the drivers could not get down, so we also stayed up. I bent low over my horse's head whenever I heard a shell coming. Frank trotted past me with a worried look on his face, it was his first time under fire since his wedding day.

'If that Jerry could shoot straight he'd wipe out the whole bloody lot of us,' one of my drivers remarked.

We waited there for what seemed a long time. Then the Major said we were doing no bloody good where we were and he wasn't going to stay on this bloody track a minute longer, not for anybody. He ordered the guns to take up a firing position on the right hand side of the road, and when this had been done he sent Frank back with all the teams and wagons. 'Go back about half a mile,' I heard him say. There was still a possibility that we might have to advance later in the day.

All the other guns on the road seemed to have come to a similar decision, and soon the road was empty. We ate our lunch in a trench. Only cold bully. The Major washed his down with a good deal of whisky, he was working himself up into a battle temper.

Then we saw an orderly galloping along the track, up from the wagon lines—Frank had been wounded, he said. Jack was our senior subaltern, but he was out in front, the Major had sent him to find out what was happening. So he told me to go and take charge of the wagon lines. 'Don't go a bloody yard back,' he said.

But the place was impossible, I found. It was being shelled with gas as well as high explosive, three drivers had already been hit besides Frank, and some horses killed. I galloped up to the gun position again and told the Major we should have no horses left to make an advance unless he allowed me to take them further back.

'It's always the same,' he said irritably. 'Put a man in charge of the wagon lines, and he's never happy till he's taken them back to the sea.' But in the end with a bad grace he agreed to let me take them half a mile further back.

So I was by myself on the night after our great attack. It was cold and the rain had begun, summer had gone, winter had come in a day. I was sleeping in the open, but I hardly slept at all. I was kept awake by German shells as well as the cold, and by the restlessness of the horses in the lines. They were tethered close, so that they could not kick one another, but the noise of the shells was frightening them. I was afraid they might break free or that a shell might burst in the middle of them, and the Major would certainly say it was my fault.

But I could have endured it all, loneliness and cold, shells and responsibility, I should not have minded anything if we had succeeded. It was the failure of all our hopes, that was what I could not bear. The Promised Land! We were practically in the same place where we had started. The Hindenburg Line was impregnable, we should never get through.

In the morning Cherry was still saying it was all right. He said that the Forty-Sixth Division had got across the canal on our right, he admitted that the Americans had been held up by the wire and had suffered very heavily, but they were sorting themselves out now, he said. I did not believe anything he said, I'd had enough of Cherry's optimism.

Twelve

October

Three mornings later, on October 2nd, we were ordered to go into action at Etricourt. 'Etricourt!' we said to one another. 'Etricourt!' Something very extraordinary must have happened. Etricourt was more than a mile across the Hindenburg Line. But there had been rumours of success the day before.

The guns had been brought back on the day after the attack to the position from which we had started. Now, at midday, we set off again. Along the same Black Road, in the same weather, a lifeless colourless day, there was no gleam in the sky.

I felt like a man in a dream.

Here was the place where the German gun had shelled us, no gun was firing now. There was the crest in front of us. We were moving steadily towards it, the road was not blocked. The head of our column was nearly there. Now the leading gun was actually going over. We were all going over. And as we came over we could see the Hindenburg Line, we were coming up to the Hindenburg Line. No one was shooting at us! Now we were going through the wire, a road had been made through the wire. Was I really awake!

Here was his front line trench, it was full of dead Germans. Now I could see the tunnel exit. And the canal, the water in a cutting below us, the steep banks. We were across, we were coming into the Promised Land.

The village of Bellicourt, where the canal came out of the tunnel, was still being shelled, not heavily, but with a sulky persistence, and a cloud of dirty-coloured smoke hung over the shattered village. But we were turning to the right, we could avoid going through the villlage. Now we were marching

118

parallel to the canal, but we could no longer see it, the cutting was too deep.

Was it real, or was I in a dream?

I was by myself at the rear of the column, I had no one to talk to. I thought of riding forward to where Durham was. If I could hear him saying, 'Pretty good, isn't it? One in the eye for the old Boche!' then I should know that it was real. But I seemed to be under a spell and without the power to leave my place, I could only ride along where I was.

I could see the Major up in front leading us, now he was turning left, away from the canal, towards the enemy again, into the unspoiled country that I had seen from the O.P., where the villages were fit to live in and the trees bore leaves. I had a sudden idea—I would come back here tomorrow. Durham would come with me; together in full daylight, not in the misty light of an October afternoon, together we would look at all this wonder. I had seen nothing like this on any other battlefield. Today it had been impossible to take it in, and we had never stopped moving. But tomorrow it would be different, we could look as long as we wanted. And at the thought of seeing the place again I began to believe that it was real, this wonder of great victory had been achieved.

But I never saw the Hindenburg Line again.

We came to Etricourt, a hamlet only, there was a belt of trees on one side. The head of the column halted a little further on. The guns were unhooked and drawn up in line, ammunition was unloaded, the teams and wagons were sent back. I was still feeling dazed.

The servants were pitching a tent under a bank. 'What's that for?' I asked Walkenshaw. 'Major's orders,' he replied. A tent in the line! It was absurd. We were not being shelled at the moment, but two German sausage balloons had been watching us. They had seen us coming in, we should be shelled soon; there was no need to sleep in a tent, with a German trench at no great distance.

But the Major said we had finished with trenches. 'It's all over, bar the shouting,' he said. 'It's come sooner than anyone could have expected. We may have heard our last shell, we shall soon forget the sound they used to make.'

So that was the way our crossing the Hindenburg Line had affected him!

Orders for the next day arrived while we were having dinner. The enemy was holding the Beaurevoir Line and we were to attack it in the morning. We were attached to the 20th Australian Battalion, and were to lay out a telephone line to their Headquarters in Estrées and then provide a liaison officer in the morning. Whose turn was it, I wondered; we had all been doing so much in the last few days. I didn't want to go. It was the hardest job in the world, laying out a line in the dark over unknown country. 'You'd better do it,' the Major said to me. Oh, damn! I got out my map and started to look for Estrées.

'I'm beginning to feel sorry for Fritz,' the Major said. 'He's put up a damned good show. I mean to say, he's had most of the world against him, and it's taken us all this time. But he's down for the count now.'

I was planning out my route. Estrées was a biggish village, only just inside our line, so far as I could make out. The Order did not give the map reference of Battalion H.Q., it merely said in Estrées, I should have to find the place when I got there. The distance was about three thousand yards. We should need a lot of wire and it was heavy stuff to carry, I should have to take four signallers with me instead of the usual two. How long would it take? I might lose my way in the dark, we might have to mend breaks if there was enemy shellfire, then I should have to find the position of H.Q. in the village. Zero Hour was at five minutes past six, I must give myself plenty of time. 'Call me at one o'clock,' I said to the signaller on duty.

'It's been a hard slog,' the Major was saying, 'but it will be downhill now for the rest of the way. We shan't stop till we come to the Rhine.'

I wished he would stop talking, I had a lot to do. Anyway, he was talking nonsense. It was absurd to suppose the war was over just because we had captured the Hindenburg Line.

I wanted to find the best way on the map and then to memorise it. There was a track marked going past the bank beside our tent, it started off in the right direction. The track bent left after a few hundred yards, towards a small wood. Should I be able to see the trees in the dark? The contours showed one would be going slightly uphill. Then the track forked, I must take the right-hand one. It led to a deep sunken lane, and the lane went all the way to Estrées, crossing a single-track railway.

'You've got nothing to worry about,' the Major told me reassuringly. 'You probably won't hear a single shell. Fritz has no guns left, we've captured them all.'

Track, six hundred yards, wood, half-right, sunken lane, railway line.

'We shall be glad not to have missed this,' the Major said. 'We're making history.'

I lay down to get some sleep. I fell asleep while the others were still talking, but woke before midnight. There was quite a heavy bombardment going on, up in the line. No German guns left! What rubbish he talked! These were German guns, and so far as I could tell the noise was coming from Estrées. I hoped it was disturbing the Major's rest, but he seemed to be breathing peacefully, I was the only one awake. Track, six hundred yards, wood, half-right, sunken lane, railway line. There was no doubt the noise was coming from Estrées, it sounded like big stuff.

It was almost a relief to hear the signaller outside. He was coming to call me. 'Nearly one o'clock, Sir,' he said. 'The signallers are waiting for you, they've got the wire.'

The darkness outside was absolute. I could see the faces of my signallers, hardly anything else. I could not even see the track where we were standing. If there was one, I lost it at once.

I set off in what I hoped was the right direction, wondering if I could keep straight, repeating the words I had memorised: six hundred yards, wood, half-right, sunken lane. At once the darkness swallowed us.

We had to go very slowly because of the weight of wire my signallers were carrying. Once or twice they called out that they could not see me, and I had to stop and let them catch up. I dared not look behind in case I lost my direction. We seemed to be going uphill. That was right, but I saw no wood.

The night was very still. I could feel a gentle breath of air on my face, and there was the sound of the shells in front. Nothing else moved or gave a sign of life. We met no one. I looked up at the sky. Not even a star to help me. But I thought it looked lighter already, low down above the enemy lines. He must know we were going to attack again in the morning, and this was why he was shelling our front-line area. The shellfire made it easy to keep straight, and we were still far enough from Estrées, where the shells were falling, to be in no real danger. By the time we were nearer to them I hoped we should be in the sunken lane and that its steep sides would protect us from flying bits.

How peaceful it was, under the wide sky! I was walking on those green hills that I had seen from the O.P. The unspoiled country! I was perhaps the first English soldier who had walked on them.

Once I should have been frightened of getting lost or arriving late at Battalion H.Q. Now everything seemed easy, the night was friendly and on my side. I was rather enjoying myself; but we ought to be nearing the sunken lane. I counted a hundred double paces, then stopped and peered ahead. My God! here it was! We had come straight to it, even in daylight I could not have found a more direct way.

It was very dark in the lane. There were trees at the top of the bank, arching across, shutting out the sky, but we came to a bridge, and that must be over the railway line, I knew. A little further on I clambered up the bank and in the red glare of the bursting shells I could see the roofs of houses, we were not more than a quarter of a mile from Estrées.

I did not intend to go any further at present. We were in very good time, and it would be madness in this shellfire to go wandering through the village looking for Battalion H.Q. Sooner or later someone was sure to come along the lane. So I told the signallers to stop and we sat down under the bank. I gave each of them a cigarette and for the first time we relaxed.

Almost at once I heard footsteps. Someone was coming along behind us. I got up and stood in the middle of the lane, waiting for whoever it was to appear. Two men came out of the darkness. They were Australians, in the 20th Battalion, they told me. It certainly was my lucky night, they were going straight to Battalion H.Q., to the very place where I had to report.

We set off with them. But though they slackened their pace a little, they were still going too fast for my signallers. I told them to stay where they were, I went on alone with the two Australians. The lane led into a trench, we went along the trench, which brought us to a dug-out at the edge of the village. This was the place, they said. They went inside, they had brought some orders for their commanding officer, I went back for my signallers, to bring them the rest of the way and finish the laying of our line.

I was feeling very pleased. It had been a difficult job, but now all my difficulties were over. We had laid our line and found the Australian H.Q., and were in communication with our own Brigade at the other end, and it was only three o'clock.

The rest would be easy.

All I had to do now was to report my arrival to the Australian battalion commander, telling him about our line and that I was to act as his liaison officer. I should have to stay with him until dusk, sending back information about the attack, shooting on any targets he might give me; but liaison work was straightforward, I always enjoyed spending a night or a day with the infantry, they were always so friendly and so appreciative of any help the artillery could give, the Australians in spite of their rough speech were no exception.

Drawing aside the gas curtain I went down some steps into the candle-lit dug-out and saluted the Colonel, who was sitting with his adjutant at a table, reading some orders, those probably which the two men had brought him, and I was aware of three or four other officers sitting or lying in the darkness at the back. I told the Colonel who I was and that I had a telephone line outside in working order. He was less welcoming than I had expected. He did not acknowledge my salute or speak to me, he hardly looked up, he went on talking in a low voice to his adjutant. I remained standing in the doorway, waiting for someone to ask me to sit down.

Presently he looked up again and this time he did speak.

123

'You'll find there's more room outside,' he said. 'If I want you, I'll send for you.'

It was like a smack in the face. I was expecting him to say we had done well to get our line up so quickly. I went back into the trench, it was shallow and dirty, I did not mind the dirt; being told I was not wanted was what I minded.

The village was still under heavy shellfire, but we were not in much danger. There was gas mixed with the high explosive, several times during the remainder of the night we had to put on gas masks. And several times also our line was broken and my signallers went out to repair it. We never had to tell our signallers to go out, they went before one knew the line was broken. I was confident of being able to tell the disagreeable Colonel that our line was in working order if he did want us in the morning.

I talked to a Roman Catholic padre, an elderly man and in appearance more like one of his men than like an officer. I wondered if there had been no room for him in the dug-out either. But clearly he did not want to be with the officers, he wanted to be with his men, they were going over the top in the morning, some of them would not be here at night, they needed the comfort he could give them. I watched him going from one little shelter to another, speaking so quietly that I could not hear what he said. I wanted to listen, but it was not my religion; I thought he might resent my presence.

The night passed very slowly. The shellfire went on, we were continually putting on our gas masks and taking them off again. There was a lot of coming and going past us in the trench. Then the Australian soldiers came out of their little holes and moved away, up the trench. I looked at my watch, it was a quarter to six, Zero Hour was at five past. I did not see the padre again and supposed he had gone up with his men. His religion was not my religion, his words would not have helped me, but his courage did. He was the first chaplain I had come across who chose to live with the men, not with the officers.

At five minutes past six all the guns behind us opened fire with a great roar. We waited, waited for the first reports to come back. They were not good when they came—the tanks had not arrived, the wire was uncut, the attack had been held up, losses had been severe. Presently I heard someone calling for the artillery officer and I was told that the Colonel wanted to speak to me. He was looking more disagreeable than ever when I went down to the dug-out again. None of the wire had been cut, he said; why didn't we ever do the job we were supposed to do?

'We only came up after dark last night, Sir,' I said. I knew there had been nothing about wire cutting in our orders, we could not have cut it in the dark.

'Always the same excuse,' he said. 'I don't know what the artillery can do,' he went on, 'they can't cut wire.'

'They can shoot us in the back,' I heard one of the others saying, 'they're very good at that.'

It was a common taunt, but I had never heard of the confirmation of any alleged case of short shooting by the field artillery, and the infantry knew as little about our difficulties as we knew about theirs.

I asked the Colonel to show me the position of the wire on his map, and then I went outside and spoke to Cherry at Brigade Headquarters. The attack had been held up, I told him, the wire had not been cut, and they were saying we ought to have done it.

'Why don't they tell us beforehand what they want?' he said.

I told him where the wire was, and he promised to put all our batteries on to it.

An hour or so later a second attack was launched and it was successful. Messages were brought back from inside the German trenches. Whether the wire had been cut by our shooting or by the tanks, which had arrived in time for the second attack, I never knew; it was more likely to have been the tanks. But anyway the news was better, most of our objectives seemed to have been captured; but there had been a lot of casualties.

For the moment there was nothing else for me to do. I ate one of my slices of bread, but I was not feeling hungry. Then one of the signallers told me he was not feeling well, and the next moment he was very sick in the trench. It was the gas, he said, gasping for breath, a gas shell had burst very close to him while he was out repairing the line. I sent him back

125

to the battery, it was quieter now, the enemy shellfire had almost ceased, we could manage without him.

Then another was sick and I sent him back also. The other two said they were all right, but they were looking green. I spoke to the Major on the telephone, told him about the sick men, and asked him to send me two fresh signallers. The other two hardly lasted until they came. All my signallers casualties! I could not understand it, the gas had been no worse than usual, there was always a smell of gas in the line, we knew when to put on our masks and when it was slight enough to be ignored, we could not be wearing our masks all the time. Besides, I had not see any of the Australians being sick.

Twelve o'clock! Six hours to wait until I was relieved! I was feeling very sleepy, I could hardly keep my eyes open, one night only without sleep should not have made me so tired. I tried to rub the sleepiness out of my eyes, but this seemed to irritate them. Well, I would give in to it, there was nothing for me to do, one of the fresh signallers could come and find me if I was wanted. I went away by myself and lay down under a hedge, where men would not be walking over me all the time, and tried to go to sleep.

But I could not sleep. My eyes had been uncomfortable when I kept them open, now they were still uncomfortable when I shut them. And my head had started to ache. I was all right, there was nothing the matter with me, it was just tiredness, and perhaps also a feeling of disappointment because at the end nothing had gone right. I thought I had done so well, it was one of the best things I had ever done, in future perhaps I need not feel such an impostor when my eye was caught by the purple and white ribbon on my tunic.

Yes, it was disappointing, but there was nothing the matter with me, nothing the matter, nothing. . . . But even as I was trying to reassure myself I knew that something was the matter. It was that bloody gas, I also had been affected by it. There must have been a pocket of the stuff lying at the bottom of the trench, some of the liquid had probably splashed against the side, we had touched it and then eaten our food, I had rubbed my eyes with my fingers. I tried walking about, my eyes were painful now, but I hoped the

126

pain would go if I was doing something. Another four hours to wait before my relief came. I must stick it out, I would not go to the unfriendly colonel and ask him to let me leave early.

But the pain grew worse. I had a terrible fear that I was losing my eyesight, not only were my eyes painful, but I could not see clearly when I tried to open them, my vision was blurred, the trench was dancing from side to side.

Two hours still, I couldn't bear it, I should have to go to him.

Feeling my way along the trench, stumbling down the steps, I went into the dug-out again and spoke to the Colonel.

'Something has happened to my eyes,' I said, 'I can't see, but I think I can wait until my relief comes if you want me, Sir.'

'Of course you must go back to your battery at once,' he said with surprising gentleness. 'I'll send one of my men with you.'

I told him this would be unnecessary.

'How will you find the way if you can't see?' he asked. I said I should follow our telephone line, holding it in my hand.

I backed to the entrance. 'You and your guns did a good job this morning,' he said as I was going out. Then I thought I heard him say, 'I ought to have seen myself that it was not cut.' The last words were not addressed to me, they may not even have been spoken, but in that moment and for the first time I was in communication with the man I have called the unfriendly colonel. I knew from others that about a dozen of his men had been killed on the uncut wire.

I set off. It was not very difficult, the line had been un-rolled along the middle of the sunken lane, I was not afraid of walking into a tree or falling into a hole. I walked slowly, as slowly as we had come up during the night. My eyes were very painful and the thought that I might never see again with them was utterly depressing. Any kind of wound would have been better than this.

When I came out of the lane and was walking in the open country there was a sudden and terrifying explosion in front of me. The shock forced my eyes open. A six-inch howitzer, hardly ten yards away, had just fired at the enemy. It had not

127

been there in the night. The gunners must have seen me, but they could not have known that I had not seen them. They looked unnaturally tall, they were dancing across the ground instead of walking, the sky was full of spots, all the trees were waving, the trees I had looked for in the night.

I went on. Now I was afraid that the shock of the gun's firing might have made me drop the line I was holding and I might have picked up the wrong one. I might now be walking in the wrong direction, not towards my own battery. In my misery I nearly stopped walking, I wanted to sit down and cry.

But I heard Durham's voice in front of me, he had come to look for me. He asked no questions, he saw that I did not want to talk, he took my arm and led me for the last few hundred yards, he helped me into a tent. 'Lie down,' he said, 'I'll take your clothes off.' He put me into my sleeping bag. 'I'll get you some tea,' he said. 'The doctor's coming round, the Major has rung up to tell him about you.'

It was wonderful to lie still, in darkness.

Our doctor came. He was a friendly young Scotsman. He gently rubbed some ointment on my eyes, which soothed them, easing the pain. 'What about it?' he said. 'Shall I send you to hospital?'

'Am I going blind?' I asked him.

'No,' he said. 'You'll be as right as rain in a few days, there's no damage done, but I'll send you to hospital if you like.'

But there was no need for that if I wasn't going blind. I only wanted to be left alone now, not to have to talk. 'I shall be all right in the morning,' I said.

I thought I should be, but I had a most unpleasant night, I hardly slept at all. There were guns all round us, firing all through the night, and every time that one fired the shell seemed to pass through my head. I was unhappy as well as in pain, the day that had begun so well had ended disastrously. All my signallers were casualties, they had all gone away. We were unlikely to get them back; they would be sent to another battery, as happened when a man was wounded. Sometimes when an officer was wounded. I wouldn't risk it, I would stay where I was, I did not want to go among strangers.

The doctor came again in the morning. 'What about it?' he said. But I told him I should be all right in a day or two. I only wanted to be left alone, and in darkness. But I could not be left where I was, for the battery was under orders to move forward again. 'I can send you to Headquarters' Wagon Lines,' he said. They were still on the other side of the canal and likely to stay there for a few days.

I was taken back in the mess-cart, and for two days I lay in semi-darkness, hardly talking, hardly eating. On the morning of the third day I was able to open my eyes and read some of the letters that had come for me, but I soon closed them again. I was content to lie there, hardly aware of anything that was happening round me. We moved once at least, I was carried in the mess-cart again.

Walkenshaw looked after me, and though I was among strangers at Headquarters' Wagon Lines I received great kindness. I did not know that men could be so gentle to other men. They told me the news—we had captured the rest of the Beaurevoir Line, and C Battery, my battery, had been bombed, a bomb had fallen on top of the mess, the Major had been wounded, the others had escaped by a miracle.

I hardly took in what they said. For the moment it was not my battery, I did not belong anywhere.

Slowly my eyes improved, but then I began coughing. The doctor said I had got some of the stuff inside me. But I should be all right, he said, I had been lucky, some people took months to recover from the effects of mustard gas.

Then Jack came to see me and he told me about the bomb. It had fallen in the mouth of their tent, the canvas had been cut to ribbons, but the tent had been dug down a foot or two and none of them had been hurt except the Major.

'We knew there was a Boche up,' Jack said. 'We had all heard the three whistles, but the Major said it was one of our own planes and he wouldn't put the candle out. "Put that bloody light out" everyone outside was shouting, and the Major was shouting back, "It's one of our own bloody planes".'

'I suppose he was telling you that Fritz had no planes left,' I said.

'Something of that kind,' Jack said. 'But what really

E*   129

annoyed him was their thinking he couldn't tell the difference between one of theirs and one of ours. Then there was this god-almighty crash, and that did put the light out.'

'Do you think he could have seen the light?' I asked.

'No,' Jack said. 'It was just a bit of bad luck. All our tents were showing up in the moonlight, he couldn't have failed to see them. I suppose you could say it was good luck really, we might all have been killed. The Major was cursing like hell in the darkness, I thought it was just bad temper, but when someone struck a match and we'd got a light again we found he'd been hit behind the ear.'

I was very sorry. We had had a lot of battery commanders, and the Major with all his faults was the man for us. We trusted him and he trusted us, and the thought of having to serve under a different commander again was very depressing. I might have given the doctor a different answer if I had known that this was going to happen.

'He'll never come back,' I said, and Jack agreed.

'You were pretty slow, weren't you?' he went on. 'All the signallers went to hospital, why didn't you?'

'I might have got down to the Base,' I said, 'but I wasn't bad enough to get home.'

'I would have been,' he said. 'I wouldn't have been able to see a thing until I saw England. By this time you could have been there and had a pretty nurse holding your hand.'

'They're not all pretty,' I said, irrelevantly.

'They're all the right sex, anyway.

Perhaps I had made a mistake. It would have been nice to be at home and to have finished with all this, at any rate for a few months. Now I should have to go back and start again, it was always an effort starting, going up to the line, knowing one would come under fire. It would be harder than usual after the gas and the days spent lying in bed so far behind the line. But it was too late now, I had made my decision, regrets were unavailing.

'How's the War going?' I asked.

'I suppose you might say it was going pretty well,' he replied. 'Mind you, it isn't over yet, we've got the hell of a long way to go still, but it's beginning to look as though we should win in the end.'

He told me they had all found souvenirs in the attack on the Beaurevoir Line. Durham had found a pickelhaube helmet and was going to take it home on his next leave.

'But I haven't much use for souvenirs,' he said. 'It's getting yourself home, that's what matters.'

Thirteen

October

It was the middle of October before I went back to the battery. The guns had come out of action for a day or two, everyone was at the wagon lines, I found two new senior officers in the mess in place of the Major and Frank. Major Ricky was a newcomer, I had never seen him before, but Captain Garnett had formerly been a subaltern in A Battery. Now he had been promoted and had come to us as our second-in-command. I knew him quite well. I had begun by disliking him, then I had learnt to like him, now I found him dislikeable again.

'Hullo!' he said as soon as he saw me. 'You all right again? Fit for full duty?'

Now I had not fully recovered and the doctor had told me that I was to do very little at first, but I had not intended to tell anyone what he said. I had intended to do as much as I felt able to, I knew that none of the others would think I was shirking if I did less than my share, they would all be willing to take some of my duties for me. But if Garnett wanted formality he should have it, I would do nothing at all. His voice sounded as though he considered I ought not to be sitting in the mess at that moment, I ought to be out in the horse lines, making up for all the time I had missed. So I told him no, I was not all right again, the doctor had said I was to do light duty only.

'Oh!' he said. He looked as though he was expecting me to bring out a medical certificate in confirmation.

He may have disbelieved me, or he may have thought he should ask the doctor for corroboration of my story, but later in the day he apologised for speaking in that way. He had not

132

realised, he said, how bad I had been; nor that I had returned to the battery at my own request.

It no longer seemed like C Battery with these newcomers in the mess, giving us orders, changing our established ways. I had been looking forward to coming home, but this was not like home, I was feeling a stranger, I got up and went outside, glad to talk to my men. They had not changed, and it seemed to me that they disliked the new faces as much as I did.

Corporal Albert came up to me with his friendly welcoming smile and asked if I was all right again.

'Yes,' I said, 'more or less. But I think I was very slow not to wangle a blighty.'

'I expect it was because you didn't want to leave the battery, Sir,' he said.

He was the first and only person who understood and did not think me stupid for refusing the opportunity of going into hospital. He was perhaps the only man in the battery whose patriotism was still as bright as on the day he joined up in 1914. He was not one of our best N.C.O.s, he did not make men do what they were unwilling to do, he believed their excuses, but for himself he had one simple principle, to serve the battery and all who were in it to the very best of his ability. Of all the officers and men in our battery, I think he was the one for whom I felt the greatest personal affection.

'We should have been sorry if you hadn't come back to us,' he said. 'We don't want to lose any more of our old officers.'

We did lose Jack. He went home on leave a few days later, and before going he took me on one side to say, 'Don't expect me back in a hurry. I've had a buzzing in my ear ever since that bomb, and I'm going to see what I can do about it. A noise of this sort ought to be worth three months at least, and six if I'm lucky.'

He never came back. I had a letter from him some time later, asking me to arrange for his kit to be sent back to England. He had not realised, he said, how bad his ears were; both the drums were ruptured.

Now Durham and myself were the only two of the old officers left.

The guns went back into action, but I did not go with

133

them, I stayed at the wagon lines. The enemy was holding a line west of Le Cateau, fifteen miles beyond the tunnel and the canal. We had won a great success, but everyone agreed that there was still a lot more fighting to be done. There were French civilians in some of the villages behind us. They had spent four years under German occupation, now we had liberated them; but liberation sometimes meant they had to leave their homes, they were in the danger zone until we drove the enemy back further.

My eyes were still bothering me and I had a troublesome cough. Garnett now was encouraging me to be lazy, he was solicitous on my behalf. 'You ought not to be out here in the rain with that cough,' he said. 'I'll take the horses down to water.' It rained nearly every day.

I could not help liking Garnett, but I was almost the only person in the battery who did. Newcomers to our battery usually began by thinking it was a bad one because it was not so smart as some others. All the older men were Territorials, they thought for themselves, they had not been trained to instant obedience, our senior N.C.O.s were in the habit of expressing their opinions. Major Eric had always listened to what they had to say and had sometimes taken their advice, but Captain Garnett threatened to put my Sergeant Denmark under arrest when he started to argue with him.

'The man was insubordinate,' he said, when I protested afterwards. 'He needs a sharp lesson.'

'Have you noticed his D.C.M.?' I asked.

'Of course I have, but it isn't always the best men who get the medals.'

Garnett and I each had one, so we could agree about this, but I had more to say. 'He got it before I came out,' I said, 'but from what I've been told it might have been a V.C. He's the bravest man in the battery, and now that Major Jack is dead I would rather have Denmark with me in a tight corner than anyone else in the brigade. For my part,' I added, 'I always take his advice.'

Garnett thought it was wrong for an officer ever to take a sergeant's advice, or even to listen to it, but he knew that I knew more about the men in C Battery than he did, and he was beginning to respect some of my opinions.

134

'Well, I'll remember what you've said about the fellow,' he conceded. 'But he's a difficult man, he's asking for trouble. The fact is that the discipline of the whole battery has been allowed to get slack and now needs tightening up.'

I then went to tell Sergeant Denmark that Captain Garnett had a lot of good qualities of which he was not aware.

'I'm certainly not aware of them,' Denmark said.

I told him Garnett was a very brave man with a very high sense of duty. 'He's got an unfortunate way of talking,' I said. 'That's all.'

'He'll get a bullet in the back one of these days,' Denmark said, 'unless he learns to talk civil.'

He was so angry that I was alarmed. 'Don't be a fool,' I said. 'You would never do anything so daft.'

'I didn't say *I* would,' was his answer.

I was very upset. Garnett was even more unpopular than I had supposed, it seemed as though he might do as much harm to the battery as Bingley had in the spring. I tried to go about with him as much as possible when he was walking in the horse lines, hoping that my presence might sometimes prevent his speaking to the men in the way they so much disliked.

I had told Denmark that Garnett was a very brave man, and he had been, at Ypres in the previous year. He had seemed not to know what fear was, but he knew now. Once he had appeared to be indifferent to shellfire, now he jumped at the sound of a pip-squeak a quarter of a mile away.

Then one night in our tent before going to sleep he told me about a girl he had met in England during the summer, he had fallen in love with her, she was everything that was wonderful; and though he was altogether undeserving of such good fortune, he said, yet for some miraculous reason she loved him and they were going to get married.

So that was why he jumped at the sound of a pip-squeak in the next field. He admitted it, he was ashamed of his cowardice, he said; but if I only knew what it was like to be in love with a girl of that sort, I should understand.

I was the first person in the brigade he had told about her, he said. He would have liked to talk about her all night. She had every virtue. She could ride better than he could and

135

was as good at games. 'I've always had a pretty good opinion of myself,' he said, 'but she's made me realise how little right I have to.' She was a vicar's daughter and was as good as she was beautiful. He had given up swearing because she did not like it. 'She gave me the hell of a blasting once,' he said, 'because I let out an oath when we were playing golf. She'll have me teaching in her Sunday School before I know where I am.'

'I expect she's a very gentle person,' I said. It had suddenly occurred to me that I might be able to make use of her, I might be able to persuade him that she would not like his talking to the men in the way that he did.

'Oh, no,' he said. 'She puts me in my place all right. She's only a girl, nearly ten years younger than I am, but she stands no nonsense from me.'

I hoped she had a sense of humour as well as every other good quality. I thought she would need it.

He woke me up one night to listen to some bombs. The bombers came over on most fine nights, and the wagon line area also was shelled by a long-range gun. Personally I found bombing easier to endure, an aeroplane carried a limited number of bombs and had to go back when they were all dropped, but a gun might go on firing all night.

Garnett disliked both equally. He had got out of bed and was standing in the doorway of our tent, telling me where he thought each bomb had fallen. 'We must dig our tent further down,' he said, 'I don't fancy being killed when the war has got to this stage.' With a little encouragement from myself he would have gone outside to look for a spade and started digging at once.

We were on the move again. Le Cateau had been captured, it was the biggest town I had seen in the middle of the fighting area and almost undamaged. The wide tree-lined streets, the squares and big houses, the names of faubourgs and hotels all combined to give an air of unreality to what we were doing. It was natural to fight among trenches and shell-holes, but altogether wrong in the middle of a town like this. It might have been our own home. I saw a dozen engines outside the railway station, looking all ready to set off with their trains behind them, and the big church with its tall spire looked ready for a congregation to come and worship. But there were dead Germans still lying in the streets.

There was a huge mound of coal near the station, but no food for us in any of the shops. There was no supplementary food to be found anywhere, we had left the canteens far behind us, we had to live on our rations. I spent a lot of my time riding round the country, trying to buy whisky for the mess, chocolate and cigarettes for the men, but I obtained very little of anything.

I was happy. I was feeling well again at last, we were winning the war, Garnett was beginning to find good in us and Major Ricky was a good battery commander, he gave his orders quietly and was steadier than the Major had been. And I had been up to the line and under fire again, I had done my first duty since returning, it was neither easy nor safe, but it had been successfully carried out and I had felt no more frightened than usual, the gassing and the night at Estrées had not made it harder for me.

Then suddenly, in a moment, all my happiness vanished. Durham came riding down from the guns one afternoon, and he said he had come to congratulate me. I looked at him uneasily, for Durham had a sense of humour that I did not always appreciate, he might be going to say that I had been chosen to go out as Forward Observing Officer with the infantry in our next attack or was to go on a gas course.

'Oh, haven't you heard?' he said. 'You've been promoted and are going to A Battery as their captain.'

I did not believe him, I thought it was part of a silly joke.

'Of course I'm being serious,' he said. 'It was in Orders this morning, we thought you would know all about it.'

I did not want to be a captain, the thought of leaving C Battery was utterly hateful, I had not a single friend in A Battery now except Major Cecil, and I knew he was disliked by everyone there, he was even more unpopular in A than he had been with us when he was our battery commander in the summer.

'I shan't go,' I said. 'They can't make me.'

'Of course you will go,' said Garnett, who was sitting in the mess with us. 'A soldier has got to obey orders.'

I went away by myself and sat down in our tent. I felt more wretched than ever before. It seemed to me that I had been happier during the last year than at any other time in my life because I had been given a man's work to do, and in the end I had learnt how to do it. C Battery had shown me how to, I loved the men who had helped me, they had given me confidence in myself, and now I was to leave them and go among strangers. I had chosen to stay instead of going into hospital when I was gassed because C Battery was my home, I could not be happy anywhere else until the War was over.

But besides this, I did not want to be a captain, I was not ready for promotion. I knew that I was a reasonably good subaltern by this time, I could do O.P. work and liaison duty as well as anyone else, I could read a map and work out the targets for our guns. But the captain's job in a battery was altogether different, he was responsible for the horses and for supplies, and for all the men down at the wagon lines, he had to move and feed the battery. If he made a mistake, if he chose a bad position for his wagon lines, it was not only his own life he put at risk but those of the hundred men under him. I dreaded the responsibility.

I sat for so long in the tent that the light had begun to fade before I moved. The afternoon was over, Durham had ridden back to the guns, I had let him go away without speaking to him again, he had probably thought that the news he brought would be pleasing to me. Garnett was alone in the mess when I went back. He talked to me as usual that evening, but I was not listening to what he said.

I should have to go. It was no good trying to escape. For a moment I had thought of making use of my eyes, they were still causing me some discomfort, I could pretend they were worse than they were, I might go to the doctor and say I wanted him to send me into hospital after all. But I should have felt ashamed of doing that, what would Corporal Albert think of me! No, I should have to go. My only hope lay in persuading Major Cecil that he had made a bad choice. If I told him that I knew nothing about horses he might decide

138

that someone else in the brigade would make a better captain for him.

I rode up to see him immediately after breakfast the next morning, but I stopped at C Battery gun line on my way. I wanted to talk to Major Ricky and I was hoping to see Sergeant Denmark also. He was the first person I saw, he came slowly towards me when he saw me.

'I hear you're leaving us, Sir,' he said.

I got off my horse so that I could talk to him more easily. 'I haven't decided yet,' I said. 'You haven't got to accept promotion.'

'If you don't, it will never be offered you again,' he said.

'I shouldn't mind, I don't want it.'

'A soldier's got to do what he's told.'

It was what Garnett had said. In some ways, not in all, they were very like each other, Garnett and Sergeant Denmark. That might be why they did not get on.

'You don't,' I said.

'What's that got to do with it?' His voice was so gruff that I thought I had annoyed him, but there was no unfriendliness in his face when I looked up.

'I don't know how to be a captain,' I said. 'I'm not good enough.'

'Who says so! You've managed all right so far, you can manage the next step too.'

'It will be so different.'

'Nothing stays the same.'

'I want it to.'

'You don't, you want to do what's right, and the right thing for you now is to be captain of A Battery.'

'All my friends are here, I don't want to leave them.'

He shrugged his shoulders. With him it was his way of indicating that his next remark would be his final one, he would have nothing further to say.

'If we've come out here to please ourselves,' he said, 'it's the first I've heard about it.'

If he thought I ought to go there was no longer any doubt in my mind, only the unhappiness remained. I rode away without looking for anyone else, I did not speak to Major Ricky, I went on to A Battery.

I felt awkward and ill at ease when I saw Major Cecil, but I told him as simply as I could that I did not think I was capable of doing a captain's job and that I was afraid I should let him down.

'That will be my funeral,' he said.

'I've not had enough experience,' I said.

'That's what the Colonel thinks, he said you were too young, but I've never thought much of his opinion. I want you because you do things, you don't just sit about.'

It would have been unfair, I thought, to say that I did not want to come to his battery, that I wanted to stay with my own; but I would say something about the horses, he was much more interested in horses than he was in guns, if I could make him think that his beloved horses would suffer under my care, then he might decide to choose someone else. It was my last hope.

'I know nothing about horses,' I said.

'I know enough for us both,' he replied.

It was very quiet in his tent. The War had become quiet, I heard the echoes of a single gun rolling along the horizon.

'All right,' I said. 'I'll do my best.'

'You'll make mistakes,' he said, 'everyone does, but I don't think either of us will regret our decisions.'

I asked for one more day, I wanted to be a subaltern in C Battery for one more day, but that evening I told Walkenshaw to sew an additional star on each of my shoulder straps and when I dressed the next morning I was a captain. The change was so great that I hardly recognised myself when I looked at my pocket shaving mirror. Walkenshaw and Edric were both coming with me, I had left the decision to them, they were both Yorkshiremen, I knew it would be hard for them to leave their friends and go among strangers. I thought that Edric looked very wistful when I gave him the choice, but with hardly a moment's hesitation he had answered, 'I'll come with you, Sir.' I was grateful to them both, now I should have two friends in A Battery.

After breakfast I went to say goodbye to my own men, all of those who were down at the wagon line. 'All the lads is sorry you are going,' Corporal Albert said, and in that moment I knew how little I had done for any of them. I might have done so much, I had done so little. But it was too late now, it was goodbye for ever.

I did not say goodbye to the men in the gun line, the men in my own Left Section and the signallers who had so often been out with me, I would see them on another day, I could not face them now, it was Sergeant Denmark I did not want to see, I did not want him to see me crying. I rode straight to A Battery wagon lines.

The Battery Sergeant-Major was waiting for me. He called the whole camp to attention as I arrived. Then he took me round the lines while the drivers were grooming their horses, calling out the senior N.C.O. as we came to each sub-section and telling me his name. All the men looked at me as I passed by. I was supposed to be inspecting them, but they were inspecting me. It was far worse than being under shell-fire.

Sooner than I had expected I began to feel at home in my new battery and to find the work less strange. Before starting there I had thought how pleased I should be if Major Cecil realised I was no good and sent me back to C Battery, but as soon as I had started I knew that this would be a most unsatisfactory solution. I was the youngest captain in the brigade and younger than any of my own subalterns, the Colonel evidently thought I was too young for responsibility, but I wanted to show him he was mistaken. I did not really like Major Cecil, but he had said that he believed in me, it would be very damaging to my confidence if he was proved wrong and the Colonel right.

Fortunately I was given a few quiet days in which to settle down. The enemy had been driven back several miles to the east of Le Cateau, but for the moment he was holding a line there, we made no attack, the batteries remained in the same position, I had a little time in which to get to know my N.C.O.s and some of the men and to learn what a captain had to do.

I worked hard, harder than ever before, now that there was no one to give me orders. I found work to do, I never stopped,

141

I had no time for reading. When I had finished today's work I began to think about tomorrow's. I was afraid of being caught unprepared. Sooner or later it was bound to happen, I was certain to be confronted with an unexpected situation, but by thinking beforehand of all that might happen I hoped to lessen the risk or at any rate the consequences of a mistake.

I saw Major Cecil every day. Sometimes he came down to the wagon lines to see how we were getting on, sometimes I rode up to the guns to find out what the news was and when the next attack was expected. He was often critical of what I had done or left undone, but his criticism was intended to be and was helpful. I liked him better than I ever had before, I even persuaded the subalterns, each of whom came down to the wagon lines in turn for a day or two, that his decisions were not invariably wrong. Finding myself in a position of authority I also found understanding of those who had been there longer than myself.

I saw a good deal of Garnett, although his wagon lines were still in the same place and I had moved mine forward, to the other side of Le Cateau. I often rode across to C Battery in the afternoon, partly for the pleasure of seeing some of my friends again, but also because it was a help to talk with another captain. We had the same problems, I liked knowing what he was going to do, and each of us could advise the other because we knew more about his battery than about our own.

I was already feeling affection for my new battery, and finding that they did some things better in A. And Garnett was finding good qualities in C, though to annoy me he would not say so. He said he had smartened them up a bit. 'The trouble is,' he went on, 'I shan't have time to make them into a decent battery, it will be all over before Christmas.'

I made a bet of fifty francs with him that it would not be. I expected to win my bet, but if I lost, fifty francs would be a small price to pay for peace.

Another great attack was to be launched within the next few days. 'Along the entire front,' Cecil had told me. I was familiar with attacks at the gun line, now I was going to find out what happened at the wagon lines when an attack was made. And

I should be alone, all the responsibility would be mine.

'One great push, and over he goes,' Garnett said optimistically.

But I was uneasy. It was when someone pushed someone else that the unexpected was likely to happen.

Fourteen

November

The attack was coming off tomorrow, the Fourth of November.

I had made my plans, I had tried to think of everything. I had ridden up to the gun line and listened to all Major Cecil's advice, together we had discussed every possibility. No definite time had been stated for the guns to advance, it was to depend on the local situation. 'We probably shan't move all day,' Cecil said. And Garnett and I had told each other what we proposed doing.

He had ridden over to see me during the afternoon, and this had saved me the trouble of going to his wagon lines to see him. Each of us thought that the other might have remembered something which he had forgotten. He stayed to have tea with me. Then, just as he was about to return, an enemy gun began shelling the valley that lay between his wagon lines and mine. If he went by the quickest way he would have to pass through the area that was being shelled, but the alternative route was two or three miles further. He stood outside the tent, looking irresolutely in the direction where the shells were falling, trying to decide which way to go.

'The trouble is,' he said, 'that I've still got a lot to do, but it seems absurd to take an unnecessary risk now.' He could not make up his mind.

'Look!' I said, 'I'd like to come with you if you don't mind, I've still got some questions to ask you. Let's go the shortest way, he'll probably have stopped shelling before we get there, and he's just as likely to switch his gun on to the other road.'

I thought he would like my company and there was not much danger, only a few shells were coming over, if we rode

144

fast when we came to the valley we might get across the danger area in between one shell and the next. In fact the shelling had stopped. I rode all the way with him to his wagon lines, then turned round and came back to my own. Garnett was more worried about shells now than I was, but I was more worried about tomorrow's attack.

'You've got nothing to worry about,' he said. 'Battles take charge of themselves, they always do. We may think we are in control, but it's quite a mistake. Nothing ever goes according to plan, that's the one thing you can be absolutely sure of.'

I had turned round and was riding away when he called after me, 'You might as well hand over that fifty francs now.'

I laughed. Christmas would soon be here, I said. I was not worrying about my fifty francs, but it was disturbing to think that nothing might go according to plan.

Well, I had done everything I could, better to try and put the whole thing out of my head now. I would have an early night and read in bed before going to sleep. That would take my mind off the attack. Sufficient unto the day!

Zero Hour was at 6.15. The noise woke me, of course, and I knew it was time to get up. The guns were close to the line, my wagon lines two or three miles further back, I was moving them up at nine o'clock.

We set off. I was moving my entire wagon lines, but we were only going half way up. If the attack had been unsuccessful there would be a considerable risk in having horses so near to the line, but if the guns were to make an advance then it would save time if the teams and limbers were already half way up. When we arrived at the place I had chosen I gave orders for the teams to be unhooked but harness to be kept on in readiness. Then leaving the Sergeant-Major in charge I rode on by myself to the gun line to find out what was happening. I might have to ride back at once and bring up the gun limbers for an advance, or leave my wagon lines where they were until further orders were received, or if it was obvious that the attack had failed I should take them all

145

back to the place we had come from. These were the three possibilities—go forward, go back, or stay where we were.

I found there was no news. This was what I had expected, there seldom was any news at first on the morning of a battle. One had to wait for news to come back. Our guns were no longer firing and the enemy reply had been very slight, we had suffered no casualties. But no one could tell us where the enemy was. Cherry said there were conflicting reports. There was no sound of firing in front, nothing to suggest that the enemy might still be close at hand. But if he had been driven back, why weren't we following him? Cherry said he had destroyed the bridges, our infantry were unable to cross the river. It sounded to me like a failure.

The morning passed. After all the excitement of our preparations it was an anti-climax. I had been half expecting to lead the battery forward into enemy territory, liberating the inhabitants, marching through another town like Le Cateau. It was certain to be an eventful day, I had thought, for we had come into a different part of France, we had left the open country behind us, now we were approaching forest land, and there were orchards all round us. We were hemmed in by trees, we could see for a few hundred yards in every direction, but no further, it was impossible even to guess what might be happening on the other side of the leafy fringe in front of us.

The morning had passed, the afternoon was passing, the short November day was slipping away, no Orders had come, there was no news. We sat on the grass behind the guns, chucking stones at a tin because we had nothing better to do.

'Well, we shan't move now,' said Major Cecil at last. 'I said we should probably stay in the same place all day. If I were you,' he said to me, 'I should take your wagon lines back to the old place, it's a better one than where they are now.'

I agreed. I sent my orderly back with a message for the Sergeant-Major, telling him to take them back. But I stayed at the gun line. I would wait for another hour, until it was dark. Orders were bound to come some time, then at any rate I should know what had happened.

They came ten minutes later. The guns were to move forward at once. To the other side of Fontaine-au-Bois, an ad-

146

vance of more than five miles in a straight line. Five miles in the dark over unknown wooded country! And full wagon loads of ammunition.

'Get them up as quickly as you can,' Major Cecil said. 'I'm going on at once, I'll leave guides for you.'

I galloped away, dreading that I might find the Sergeant-Major had already moved. I was in time. But the horses had not been watered or fed and they had this long march in front of them, the Sergeant-Major did not think they could do it without food; and the men would need something before they set off.

I trusted the Sergeant-Major. His judgement on anything to do with horses was better than mine. But I was angry with myself for not having ordered an earlier time to water and feed. Now it would be dark before we were ready to start. Walkenshaw came to ask if I would like my own dinner, but I was too impatient to eat, I could only fuss about in the lines, urging everyone to be quick.

It was after six o'clock before the guns were limbered up and ready to begin their advance. The night was very dark and the road was blocked. All the other batteries, those in other brigades as well as our own, were in front of me. When one wagon was halted, all the others behind had to halt, we were held up every few minutes. It was so dark that I could not see more than a yard or two, I could not see that the wagon in front of me had halted until I bumped into it, and then I could hear all my own guns and wagons bumping into one another. This always made drivers bad-tempered, I could hear them cursing in the darkness. I was in a bad temper too, I wanted someone to swear at, I swore at the guide that Major Cecil had left me, he confessed at once that he did not know the way; it all looked different in the dark, he said.

Then I swore at a driver in some other unit. His wagon had fallen into a shell-hole in the middle of the road, he could not get it out, we could not go past until he had. I cursed him fiercely, abusing him in terms I had never used before. I knew I was being unfair, it was not his fault that his wagon had upset in the darkness, he was only a young soldier, he could not answer me back, and I could tell that my abuse was hurting. But I was on trial, on trial as a captain, and I felt

147

that everything was working against me. Eventually he was able to pull a little to one side and we could pass him.

I knew the map co-ordinates of the place I was to go to, but that was all. Somewhere I had to turn left, but in the darkness it was very difficult to see turnings. One might go past a turning without noticing it or, worse still, one might turn where there was no turning and end up in an orchard or a garden, unable to go on or to turn round.

We were in the village of Fontaine-au-Bois, a long straggling place, all the houses were a little way back from the road, I could only see their dark shapes. All were in utter darkness, there was nothing to show whether any living person was inside them. There were dead German soldiers lying on the road. The trees made it darker still, there were so many, there seemed to be an orchard by every house. Fontaine was probably a well-to-do suburb of Landrecies, that would account for the number of trees. The bodies of the German soldiers had been dragged to the side of the road, but in the darkness it was difficult to avoid them.

I was bitterly disappointed with myself. We should be hours late, all the other batteries would be up before us, Cecil would ask me if I had made a mistake in the day, I hated his sarcasm. And we might be on the wrong road, I might have missed the turning, we might land ourselves in Landrecies. If once you got on to the wrong road in the dark with teams and wagons behind you it was almost impossible to get back on to the right one. This was the first difficult job that I had been given to do as a captain, and I was making a mess of it.

There was less transport on the road now, there was nothing immediately in front of me, but I had to go slowly because of the darkness and because I was peering to my left all the time, hoping to see an unmistakable turning. Suddenly out of the darkness in front I heard the most astonishing, the most unexpected, sound I ever heard at the War—the laughter of girls. And in the next moment out of the enveloping night half a dozen young girls came walking along the road. They jumped out of our way when they saw me, I saw one girl deliberately tread on the body of one of the Germans.

We went past them. It was all over in a few seconds, they had come out of the night, they had gone back into it. I heard nothing but the jolting of the guns and wagons behind me, the tread of horses' feet on the cobbled road. But they had been there, I had not imagined them, I had heard their young voices and seen light-coloured dresses under their dark coats. Girls in the middle of the War! On such a night, in such a place! Anxious and dispirited though I was, yet their extraordinary appearance, as it seemed, made me less unhappy. There still were girls in the world, life was not all fighting and marching, one day it would have a different and a nobler purpose. Their presence on the road was less extraordinary than I supposed, afterwards we met other French people, it had not occurred to me that they would have run away into the forest when the fighting started and were now returning to their homes.

I found the turning. We still had some way to go, but it was easier now, I knew I was on the right road and the darkness seemed less intense. The great forest was on our left, not far away, I could see its dark mass, darker than the sky above. I had to turn left again, into a narrower road, but this turning was easier to find because it was not so dark.

I found the place, I was about to turn, but there was a mounted man in the middle of the road, blocking the entrance. I recognised him, he was a bombardier in C Battery, a man I knew well.

'Excuse me, Sir,' he said. 'Captain Garnett said I was not to let anyone come along here until his wagons returned, he said the road was too narrow.'

So Garnett had got up already and was now returning. I asked how long his wagons would be, but the bombardier did not know. They might be an hour, I thought. I wasn't going to wait out here for an hour when I was so late already. Garnett ought to wait for me since his guns were up already.

'Captain Garnett can go to hell,' I said, and pushing past the bombardier I told my leading gun to follow me into the lane.

Almost at once I heard Garnett coming. We could have waited, we should not have been delayed for more than ten minutes, but it was too late now. I heard Garnett long before I could see him. He could hear us coming along the road and he began cursing us without knowing or caring who we were.

He was hoping to make us turn back, but there was no possibility of our doing so when once we had come into the lane. We might be able to squeeze past one another. If not, I did not know what would happen, we might both be stuck there for the rest of the night.

Garnett had ridden on in front of his wagons, he was obviously in a very bad temper, he started to shout at me. What the bloody hell did I mean by disregarding his orders, who the blazes did I think I was. He told me what he thought of me, he was very abusive. I felt my own temper flaring up, I was about to swear back at him. But what was the use! His voice was louder than mine and he had a far greater vocabulary of abuse. Besides, I was in the wrong, I ought to have waited, and I was too tired to start a slanging match with him in front of both our batteries. But I was very distressed, it meant the end of our friendship, and it was hard that on this night I should lose one of my few remaining friends on top of everything else.

There was room to pass, we all got by, we did not even scrape one another's wheels. There were good drivers in both our batteries. I was riding on, Garnett had gone away. Then I heard someone cantering up behind me. It was Garnett. O God, I thought, he's going to say something else! I couldn't take any more.

'I say,' he said, when he was riding beside me, 'I am sorry! I've been in a foul temper all night, I didn't mean any of the things I said, it's unpardonable to speak like that to a friend, but try to forget if you can.'

He turned round and had ridden away before I could say that it was all right. I wished that I had said I was sorry to the young driver whose wagon had upset.

We were nearly there now. Major Cecil came out to meet us. 'Whatever happened to you?' he said. 'I thought you were never coming, the other batteries have been up for hours.'

Well, we were up now. Guns and ammunition; and there had been no firing to do, so my lateness did not matter. Our return journey was easier, two and a half hours instead of six. But on the way I made up my mind that whatever the risk I was going to keep my wagon lines closer to the guns in future. I would go out in the morning as soon as it was light and find a place for them east of Fontaine-au-Bois.

I was cold and very hungry when we got back, but Walkenshaw had a meal ready for me, and afterwards I fell asleep immediately. But only for a few hours. I was up at seven o'clock and out with the Sergeant-Major, looking for a place to move to.

We found the perfect place, a big farm, with a stream and empty barns and stables. All the farm stock had been commandeered by the enemy, not only was there accommodation for the men, but we could put most of the horses under cover.

We moved immediately after breakfast, before anyone else could usurp our place. But the rain had already begun, we were wet through when we arrived at the farm. It was the first time we had occupied a place in which the owners were living, and I went into the kitchen to warm myself and dry my wet clothes.

War was strange, I reflected. Once I had thought that all battles were the same, but this year they had all been different, and the one we were fighting now was the strangest of all, not like a battle at all. Here was I drying myself by a kitchen stove while the woman the house belonged to was preparing dinner for her family, and a boy of nine or ten stood watching me from the doorway. Yesterday or the day before there had been German soldiers in his home, now he had British ones to look at. He and his family had probably run away into the forest when our attack started, like the girls I had seen the night before, and stayed there until it was safe to return. It was as though they had been playing a game of hide-and-seek, the sort of game I had played myself at the same age as this boy. But this was not a game, it was war, he or his mother might have been killed by one of our shells. All his life he would remember the day when he was caught up in the war, he might remember the wet English officer, the first he had seen, drying his clothes in his mother's kitchen.

Walkenshaw came to tell me that my lunch was ready, he had taken it into one of the other rooms in the farm. Hot stew. There was hot stew for everyone, and everyone was eating under cover, out of the rain. I was hoping that we might be left alone for the rest of the day, but before I had finished eating, an orderly came down from the guns with an urgent message from Major Cecil. Another advance. Gun limbers and first-line wagons immediately.

So out into the rain again. It took us only an hour to reach the guns, but longer to pull them out of the orchard. The heavy rain had made the ground so soft that the wheels sank in, we needed teams of ten horses instead of six and could only move one gun at a time. We had to unhook the two leading pairs of one gun team and put them in front of another team, then when that gun was out on the road, eight horses were brought back to pull the next one out.

But the task was accomplished and there was no difficulty on the road, though we had to go a long way round because the enemy had blown up a cross-roads. He had also blown up the bridge over the Sambre canal, but the Engineers had constructed another and we came into the town of Landrecies as darkness was falling. Through the town, and then for about a mile on the other side. This time there was no difficulty in finding the way and the guns were in position before seven o'clock.

Major Cecil said he had done some hard thinking while he was waiting for us. It was going to be moving warfare for the next few days, he said, and the guns would not be able to keep up unless the limbers and first-line wagons stayed with them; they would be under his direct command.

The idea of keeping horses at the gun line was hard to accept for a moment, but he said it would be quite safe, they had not been shelled all day, the other batteries were doing the same. I was to stay with the rest of the wagon lines, and he suggested that I should move each day to the place where the guns had been on the previous day.

'You'll have nothing to do,' he said, 'except to see that we're supplied with food and ammunition.' But he was going to keep all the best horses, I should have to make do with the others.

We returned to the farm at Fontaine-au-Bois, but the limbers and first-line wagons were to go up again with the Sergeant-Major as soon as it was light, I should follow later. The rain had never stopped, but I was no longer feeling discouraged. Everything had gone well today, I had become a different person. Now for the first time since coming to A Battery I felt sure of myself, I was not afraid of some unexpected occurrence, I would wait until it happened and then deal with the matter as best I could.

I had not long to wait. On the very next morning I learnt that no rations had come up during the night. A wagon had gone to draw them in the ordinary way and simply had not returned. Cecil had said that the only thing I had to do now was to feed them, and it looked as though I should fail on the first day. I knew I should be held responsible, feeding the battery was the captain's job and no excuse for failure was ever accepted, but I was not greatly worrying.

The wagon eventually arrived, and I sent up the day's rations immediately. The midday meal would be late, no other harm had been done. I then rode up myself to find out where the guns were going to. They had already moved, three miles further on. I followed them. 'I wonder you dare show your face,' Cecil said, when he saw me. I told him I had come to have lunch with them. 'Well, you've got some cheek,' he said, 'you eat all our rations at the wagon lines and then expect to share the little we've got left.' He told the servants to give me very small helpings.

Afterwards I rode back to meet my wagon lines, which were coming up from Fontaine, I had told the subaltern who was there to move after the midday meal. I would meet them, I said, by the bridge before Landrecies. The rain had never stopped, I never saw Landrecies in the dry, it looked a depressing place. But what was not depressing was the sight of a field outside the town full of captured guns. There were so many that it really seemed possible now that the enemy had none left on our part of the front. At the gun line they were beginning to say they had forgotten when they last heard the sound of a German shell.

This went on for some days longer. So did the rain. I almost lived in the saddle. Immediately after breakfast I rode up to the gun line to learn what the news was and where they were going that day. Then I had to find the easiest way to bring my wagon lines up. The shortest way was not always the best, low-lying places by the rivers were sometimes under water after so much rain, it was better to go an extra mile, or up an extra hill, than run the risk of being stuck in flood water. I had to go along every road myself to make sure it had not been mined, and that the bridges were all right. I knew that my horses were being used to the limit of their strength and that unless I spared them every unnecessary effort they might not be able to go on.

Sometimes we seemed to be the only soldiers left in the war. Where all the others were I did not know, I never saw them. Sometimes we were the first to be seen by the liberated French people. In the courtyard of one farm where we stopped for a few hours an elderly man came up to me and seized my hand. I thought he would never let me go, words poured out of him and tears down his weather-beaten face. I was on my horse, he was standing beside me, looking up at me with an emotion which at first I hardly understood. I did not know what he was saying, I wanted to say something to him, but I knew no French, I had not troubled to learn it at school. How could I have foreseen the day when an old Frenchman would be thanking me for saving his country!

He stopped at last, he let go of my hand, but he was still looking up at me, he was waiting for me to say something in reply. What could I say! 'Vive La France!' I said, lightly touching his bare head with my fingers, 'Vive La France!' In the end I was nearly as moved as he was.

In another farm I asked for permission to put our horses in the empty barns. 'Permission?' said the woman in amazement. 'You ask for permission?' They would have allowed us to do whatever we wanted, they would have given us everything they had. They were disappointed that I would not sleep in their own bedroom, they cleaned the outhouses where our men were. They were not fit for English soldiers, they said.

There was no time to think about the war, I had too much to do. But sometimes I wondered if it might be coming to an end. Strange things were certainly happening. We met returning prisoners-of-war on the road one day. Italians, they told us they were. Their clothes were in rags, they were cold and hungry. Our drivers stopped on the road and gave them some of their own rations, they could always understand the people of another country.

154

The war had become hushed, it was unlike anything I had known before. Or anyone else. But there was no news about it, we did not see any newspapers, they could not keep up with us. More serious was the fact that our mail often failed to come up.

It might be coming to an end, but no one could be sure. It had happened before that one side or the other had retreated a long way, and had then stopped retreating, and the fighting had begun again, shells and the noise of battle, and casualties, everything as before. This would probably happen again, I thought; it was the most likely thing.

The rain went on. I seemed to have been riding to and fro across France for a lifetime, but in fact it was less than a week since the battle had begun.

Fifteen

November 10-11

Then one morning I was awakened early, before it was light, by someone calling my name, but I had been so deeply asleep that I could not answer at once. It was not only because of my deep sleep that I could not answer, I did not know where I was, nothing looked familiar. Then I remembered. Of course! We were sleeping in houses now, not tents, I was in an upstairs room, I remembered the noise my boots had made coming up the stairs the night before. The man who had called my name was down below.

He called again. 'Hello!' I managed to answer. Then I heard someone coming slowly up the stairs. 'I'm here,' I called out, and he came into the room. It was an orderly with a message from Major Cecil, I was to go up to the gun line at once. I asked the man if he knew why I was wanted, but he could not tell me.

In five minutes I was ready to go. Walkenshaw brought in his usual mug of morning tea, hot strong and sweet, leaves floating on the surface, as I was wrapping my puttees round my legs. 'You've been quick,' I said. 'How did you boil the water?' All the world had been asleep a few minutes before. He only replied with a grin and I guessed that Madame had provided the boiling water. If the French people as well as our servants were going to look after us in future, it would be a more comfortable war.

I found Edric waiting with our horses outside the house, and we set off, trotting along the road up to the guns. The sun was just rising. The rain had stopped at last and the sun had come back. No wonder I felt happy! It had taken me a minute or two to realise the cause of my happiness, but it was the sun of course. I saw its reflection in the puddles on the road, and there were flashes of light, now green, now red, from raindrops in the hedge as we passed by. It was the first time we had seen the sun since our attack started; only a week ago, but so much had happened.

I broke into a canter, because of the beauty of the morning, not because I thought there was any need to hurry. I could not believe there was any urgent reason for my early-morning summons, war had not begun again, there was no sound of battle in front. I was not even listening for the sound of a shell or the sudden stabbing burst of machine-gun fire. How quickly it had changed! A week ago I should certainly have been listening, we were always listening, always ready to jump off our horses or dive into the nearest hole. Now I could be thinking only of the loveliness of the morning as I rode up towards the line.

How beautiful the trees were! Autumn was just as beautiful as spring. Last spring there had been all that anxiety, every morning we had been expecting the enemy to make his next attack. Now there was nothing to dread, nothing even to think about at the moment. I was out riding in the country on this perfect morning and I was twenty years old. Only another month of being twenty, I must make the most of it.

How beautiful the country was! As beautiful as England! This might have been a southern county of England, woods and low hills and a stream in the valley below. It was like places in England that I knew, but more exciting because it was unknown country, every bend in the road showed me a view I had never seen before.

In England I should not have been riding a horse. Soldiers could ride for pleasure, but an ordinary person had to be rich to ride in England. I leaned forward and stroked the neck of my mare. I was very fond of her, and proud of her good looks, I enjoyed being the envy of other officers in the brigade.

No one else was about, Edric and I had the beauty of the morning to ourselves. I slowed down and waited for him to catch me up. We walked side by side. 'This sort of war's all right,' I said, and I remarked on the prettiness of the country. 'Like England,' I said.

157

But Edric did not think much of it. 'Give me Ilkley Moor,' he said.

'Is it true, Sir,' he asked presently, 'that Jerry has sent envoys to ask for peace?'

I had heard the rumour. For two or three days past the air had been thick with rumours, they came up from the rear with the ration cart.

'I never believe these rumours,' I said. 'Then I'm not disappointed when they turn out to be false.'

But Edric thought there might be something in this one. 'It sounds to me as though Jerry has stopped fighting,' he said, 'and if once he stops he may find it difficult to start again.'

Then he began telling me what he wanted to do when he got back to Civvy Street. He was going back to the Railway on which he had served for a few years before joining up, now he would be a cleaner, he said, then a fireman, and at last if all went well a fully-trained driver.

I should have expected him to do something with horses, for he knew a lot about them and was a good groom. But he said there would not be any horses left in the country in ten years' time. He had evidently been thinking about his future, but I had not begun to think about mine.

We came down to the rushing stream. All the rivers were in flood and flowing fast. We stopped for a moment on the bridge to watch the swirling eddies, running water had a fascination for me. Then up again steeply on the other side, and the guns were on the road at the top.

Everyone at the gun line had gone back to sleep, and Major Cecil had forgotten why he had sent for me. Slowly he yawned himself awake. Then he told me that he thought the time had come to join up the two parts of the battery. He said he was expecting orders to move the guns forward again before midday, but if I brought my wagon lines up as soon as the men had finished breakfast I might catch up with them before they moved.

I was pleased at the idea, it really would make my work easier if we were all together and I should enjoy having the company of the others, for I had generally been alone during the last few days. I rode back at once, quickly gave the necessary orders, and we were ready to move in good time.

But we were too late, the guns had already gone forward. Not so far as usual, however, only two miles, to a position on the other side of the main road from Avesnes to Maubeuge, and Cecil had left a message telling me to follow them.

It was not a long march, but it was a difficult one. The road on which we were had been blown up on both sides of us, we had to go off the road and along an unmetalled lane, over some soft fields, across another stream and then up on to the main road. It was the kind of march I had been trying to avoid all these days and I was afraid that some of my horses might fail me. But it was all right, they pulled better than I had expected, and all the men were in good spirits, either as a result of the change in the weather or because of the rumour that German envoys had come to ask for peace.

I thought our difficulties were over when we got on to the main road, but there was still one more, or one more anxiety. We had to march along the road for half a mile or so before turning east, and at the point where we turned I saw some sappers digging by the side of the road. They were looking for a mine, they told me. A mine had been reported by some French civilians, they thought one was there, and if it was it might go off at any moment.

The civilians were right. Later in the day I saw the mine, it had been found and defused, but I had a few uneasy minutes as we went by. Half a mile further along the road I caught up with the rest of the battery. They were in a first-rate place, there was sufficient accommodation for all of us, the horses under cover and the men in barns. Cecil said he supposed we should be going on again, by tomorrow morning at the latest. But even one night's rest in a place like this would do us all a world of good.

Cherry came to see us in the afternoon and he thought we might have more than one night. We were in front of all the other batteries, he said, and in front of most of the infantry too. 'You've moved fast,' he said, 'but the Boche has moved faster still, he's winning the race, he's back at the Belgian border already.'

'What's going to happen then?' Cecil asked.

'It's all over,' Cherry told us. 'Fritz has had enough, he's

159

legging it for all he's worth back to his own country, we shall follow at our own speed, a triumphal march to the Rhine.'

The trouble with Cherry, as always, was that you did not know how much to believe of what he said; how much might be fact, known to him because as adjutant he saw all the information from Divisional and Corps Headquarters, how much was fancy, the result of his incurable optimism. It might well be true that the enemy was already back at the Belgian border, only five or six miles away, but had he any reason for saying he was legging it back to his own country, how could he know what was in the mind of the German commanders.

They lived in a world of make-believe at our Brigade Headquarters. If they wanted to believe something they stated it as a fact, it had always been like this, they were never abashed when the truth turned out to be altogether different.

In the morning Major Cecil rode off to Headquarters to find out whether or when we were to advance. 'Have everything ready for a move,' he said to me, 'but don't harness up.' Some time later I saw him returning, riding fast, and carrying something in his hand. He waved it at me, whatever it was that he was carrying, when he saw me.

'Read that,' he said, when he came to where I was standing.

It was an envelope, an ordinary envelope, addressed in Cherry's handwriting to the O.C. A Battery. It was only orders for the day, but when I opened the envelope I saw there was only a single sheet inside, instead of the usual sheaf of papers. I opened it and read:

'Hostilities will cease from 11.00 hours today, November 11th.'

'What does it mean?' I asked him.

'The War's over,' he said.

'Do you believe it's true?'

He said there was no doubt about it. The Germans had surrendered, the official news had come through while he was at Headquarters, he had only waited for his copy of the order, and had then galloped back to show it to us.

I looked at my watch. It was ten o'clock already, there was no possibility now of any of us being killed.

'We'll fire a salvo of blank at the right time,' Cecil said, and he rode away to give the order and tell everyone what had happened.

I felt excited, and happy, but in an uncertain subdued way. I did not want to shout or to drink; there was nothing to drink, anyway. I wanted to be with my friends, but none of those of my own age was left in the brigade. Durham had gone home on leave before the attack started, Vernon was in South Africa. There had not been time yet to become intimate with any of the other officers in A Battery or with any of the new ones who had come to the brigade in the last few months. I felt alone, I walked about in the lines but without going anywhere.

At a few minutes before eleven o'clock we all went to where the guns were, drawn up in line behind a hedge. The gunners were in their places, the rest of us standing about, singly or in little groups, behind them. Major Cecil was standing on the left of the line, by Number One gun, he was holding the big battery watch in his left hand and a whistle in the other. He's trying to make it seem like Zero Hour, I said to myself, but he can't, it's not real.

I heard him blow the whistle and all the guns fired. They fired again. Three times altogether. This was the first time I had heard our guns firing blank ammunition. It was not the proper sound, there was no report, as there would have been with live shells. The noise was no more than a bang, and puffs of white smoke hung over the muzzles of the guns and drifted slowly away. Some of the men started to cheer, but their voices sounded as unnatural as the noise of the guns, and they soon stopped. There was Silence. It had come to stay.

We drifted towards the mess.

'O God! what a war!' Cecil said 'Nothing to drink but lime juice. What a peace!'

The other batteries were in the same condition, there was not a drop of whisky in all the brigade.

'What on earth are we going to do with ourselves now?' someone said.

'Work, for a change,' Major Cecil told him.

'They won't pay us for doing nothing.'

'I know,' another suggested, 'they'll use us to tidy up the battlefield.'

161

In the afternoon I went for a ride with Cecil and we visited some of the other batteries. Everyone was excited, everyone was talking about the wonderful thing that had happened, but there was an air of constraint, everyone was talking loudly, but no one had anything to say. I gave Garnett the fifty francs I owed him, he did not want to take it, he said it had not been a fair bet, it had been obvious all along that I should lose.

Even Cherry was less cheerful than he had been on the previous day. The idea of a triumphal march to the Rhine was off, he said, so far as we were concerned, only the divisional artillery was going. 'They don't want the army brigades,' he said, 'now the fighting is over.'

The Colonel was planning a great re-union of the brigade for next spring. 'A real slap-up affair,' he said. 'Wives and sweethearts as well. In Bolton or Blackburn. For everyone who's ever served in the brigade, we'll do the thing in style.'

The Colonel was a wealthy man and I knew that he would spare no expense to ensure the success of his party, but what was the use of a slap-up affair some time next year! A slap-up affair now, that was what we needed, and what chance was there of our having any affair at all in this lonely corner of North-Eastern France! Besides, Bolton or Blackburn, he had said. That was where the Colonel himself and most of the men in the brigade came from, but I could not think our Yorkshiremen in C Battery would thank him or take the trouble to go, Sergeant Denmark would not be there.

That night we played cards, vingt et un. It was the first time I had ever thought of such an occupation, always before there had been a more worth-while way of passing an evening, but someone suggested it, and there was nothing else to do, we were in need of some excitement. But the excitement was not genuine, it was no more genuine than the sound of the guns had been in the morning.

We continued playing until midnight. Then the others went off, they were sleeping in another house, Cecil and I were left alone. We went outside to relieve ourselves. The sky was full of stars, there was no wind.

'Perfect night for bombing!' Cecil said.

'Do you think it's real?' I asked.

'Listen!' he said.

I could hear some of our horses on the other side of the farm, but no other sound. There had never been a night like this. We could hear the silence, it was a little frightening, we had forgotten what silence was.

We stood there for a minute or two without speaking, then went back into the house and into the room where we were sleeping. Slowly we began to undress. We could take all our clothes off tonight, it would be pyjama warfare for all the rest of time.

'It's been a bit flat,' Cecil said. 'I don't know what I was expecting, but certainly not this.'

We got into our beds, but left our candles burning beside us. Cecil began telling me about his plans. He said there was an empty chateau half a mile along the road, no one was living in it. 'We'll go and have a look at the place in the morning,' he said, 'and if it's as good as they say, arm-chairs and chandeliers and four-poster beds, we'll move in.'

I hope he would not want to move. We had everything we needed here.

'I was having a look at the country when we were out this afternoon,' he went on. 'We'll put up some jumps, we'll be able to make a first-rate steeplechase course.'

I was not such an enthusiastic rider as he was, but I agreed that it was a good idea, there had been no steeplechasing in the brigade since the beginning of the year.

'And we must see about a football pitch for the men,' he said, 'they've had no football for donkeys' years.'

He lit another of his Turkish cigarettes and offered one to me, but I had been smoking all evening. 'I'm even running out of these things,' he said. 'I must get my wife to send me out some more. And we ought to see about getting some Gold Flake for the men. Cigarettes for the men and whisky for ourselves, these are really the two most urgent things.'

I promised to ride into Avesnes the next day to see whether any canteens had come up, but I was not very hopeful. Everything was scarce, we had not seen an egg for weeks past.

'You know, it's not going to be all that easy,' he said presently. 'We may be stuck here for months with nothing to do. Football's all very well, but we shall have to think up other ways of keeping the men out of trouble.'

163

This was a new idea to me. Keeping them out of the way of shells, that had been our business in the past, it had not occurred to me that we should merely change one responsibility for another.

'Battery sports,' Cecil said. 'Mounted and unmounted, tent-pegging, competitions for the best turned-out team, and the best driving. We're lucky to have our horses, there's a lot you can do with horses, we may even be able to think of something to do with the guns.'

For some minutes we were both silent. I wasn't ready for sleep yet, but I thought we had said enough about immediate plans. I realised with some surprise that Cecil would be a better battery commander in peace time than he had been in war.

'You know,' he said, 'I rather envy you going up to Oxford.'

Oxford? I wasn't going up to Oxford. To go back to school after all this!

'I never did a stroke when I was up,' he said, 'but you may want to.'

It might be a good idea to go up for a term or two, it would give me time to think what I wanted to do.

'I had a wonderful time there, the best time of my life. There's so much to do, polo, point-to-points, clubs, commem balls.'

These were not the things I should want to do if I did go up to Oxford. Anyway, I couldn't afford them, I wasn't a rich man's son.

'Oxford's just the place for you,' he went on. 'You're cut out for Oxford, it will suit you down to the ground.'

I did not think it would. I could not imagine myself going back to text books and working for exams. The army had suited me. I had enjoyed being one of a team, I should feel lonely at Oxford on my own.

'You weren't cut out for this sort of thing,' he said.

I felt a little annoyed. It seemed to me I had been all right at this sort of thing. I thought I had done as well at war as I was ever likely to do at peace. 'I don't think any of us were cut out for it,' I said. 'It didn't come naturally to any of us.'

He agreed that we had all found it hard at first, but some

164

were more out of their depth than others. 'I can't read a book,' he said, 'but you're always reading. You feel at home with books.'

I didn't. I had felt at home in C Battery, now I was beginning to feel at home in A. I was at home when I was with people I liked, books were only a substitute.

'You will have forgotten all about this after a term or two at Oxford,' he said. 'You'll have forgotten there ever were places called Heudecourt and Villers Bretonneux.'

How could I forget! They were the real places, Oxford was the dream one.

'But we may not forget,' he said, a minute or two later. 'There have been good times mixed up with the bad ones. We may want to talk about them if we ever see one another again.'

If we ever see one another! Of course we should see one another, you did not give up your friends just because a war had come to an end.

I wanted to stop talking now and to be alone with my thoughts, he had given me a lot to think about, Oxford and after-Oxford and seeing my friends. I waited for a pause, then blew out my candle.

'Good night,' I said.

'Whisky and cigarettes then, those will be your priorities,' he said.

They certainly were not. But I would go into Avesnes, I should enjoy being by myself, I should have some time for thinking. One of my priorities in the morning would be to write home to my parents, to tell them I was still alive. I knew how anxious they had been ever since I came out, but I had not felt able to write at once, I had not known what to say. It had never been difficult to write to them before, except when there was no time, but today it would have been.

I had not begun to think about it until now, but the prospect of after-Oxford disconcerted me. I did not know what I wanted to do, I had no ideas. I had learnt how to do this job and could have gone on doing it indefinitely, war had been easy, once you got into the way of it. But the thought of having to make another fresh start, of going out into an unfriendly world. . . . The world was unfriendly, it did not care

165

what happened to you. That would be the difference I should find in after-Oxford. Here, everyone was on the same side as yourself, wherever you went, unless you went a long way back, you could be sure of receiving help when you needed it. But there, it would be a case of everyone for himself.

'I suppose you might say that we have been the lucky ones,' Cecil said.

I thought he was asleep. I pretended that I was, I did not answer him, I was trying to get some of my ideas sorted out, I was afraid he might begin talking about whisky and cigarettes again.

Perhaps it would turn out all right. I would go up to Oxford for a year or so anyway. That would give me time to adjust myself to the new way of living. I should miss all this friendship, but I should enjoy reading again, and History was about people.

It would be all right. Life was less difficult than you expected it to be. The War itself had seemed very difficult in anticipation and I had been very afraid. Not only of danger, but of failing. That first morning when I heard the guns. The noise had been utterly terrifying, though I was in no danger at all, the guns and the shells were miles away.

The sound of gunfire! Heard for the first time on a spring morning, and for the last on a November afternoon. I should never hear it again, there would never be another war like this one. The Last War in History! Well, even if I achieved nothing else in life I had done something, I need not feel my life had been altogether wasted, I had played my part.

The lucky ones, Cecil said we were. I found myself thinking about the others. Now we should become aware of their loss, we had hardly done so until now, we had still been with them, in the same country, close to them, close to death ourselves. But soon we should have to go away and leave them, we should be going home, they would stay behind, their home was in the lonely desolation of the battlefield. Thirty miles of lonely desolation! From Villers Bretonneux to the Hindenburg Line.

But it had not seemed lonely on the day I was there, I had not felt alone in the middle of the desolation, though darkness was beginning to fall. No one else was there, only the

166

driver of the lorry which was carrying me across, and we had not spoken to each other. *They* were everywhere. If I had been able to see and hear them I could not have been more conscious of their presence.

No, they would not be lonely, there were too many of them. I saw that bare country before me, saw it again in the darkness of the room where we were lying, the miles and miles of torn earth, the barbed wire, the litter, the dead trees. But the country would come back to life, the grass would grow again, the wild flowers return, and trees where now there were only splintered skeleton stumps.

They would lie still and at peace, below the singing larks, beside the serenely flowing rivers. They could not feel lonely, they would have one another. And they would have us also, though we were going home and leaving them behind. We belonged to them, and they would be a part of us for ever. Part of us for ever, nothing could separate us.

'Yes, we've been the lucky ones,' I said to Cecil.

But he was asleep.